Color Utopia

a unique mandala coloring experience

Handcrafted by Emily Collison

I0511204

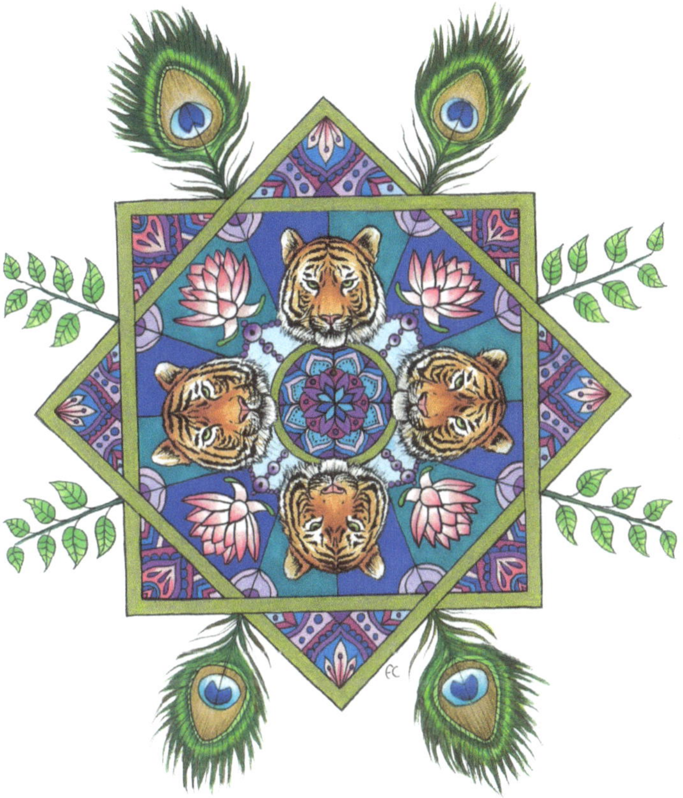

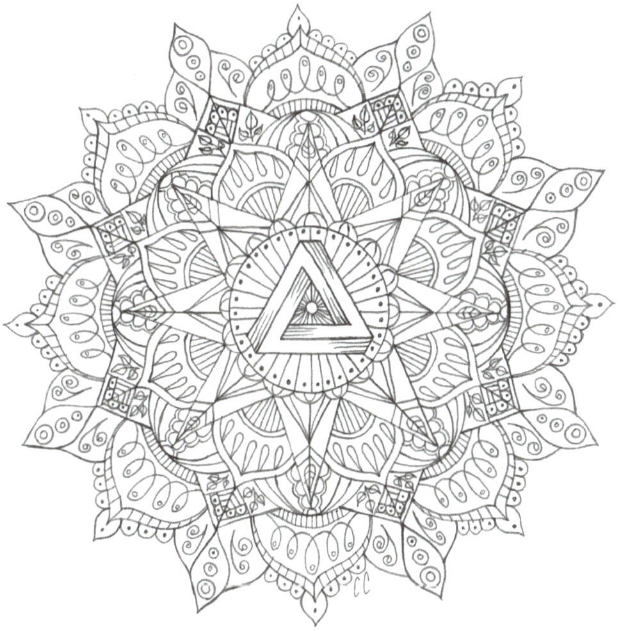

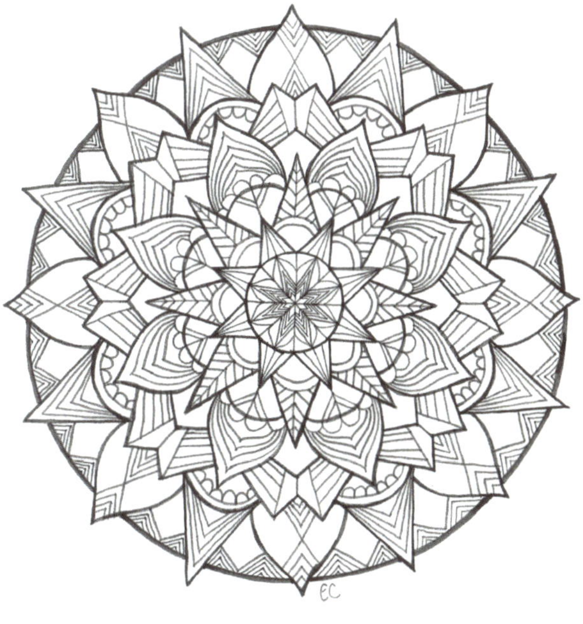

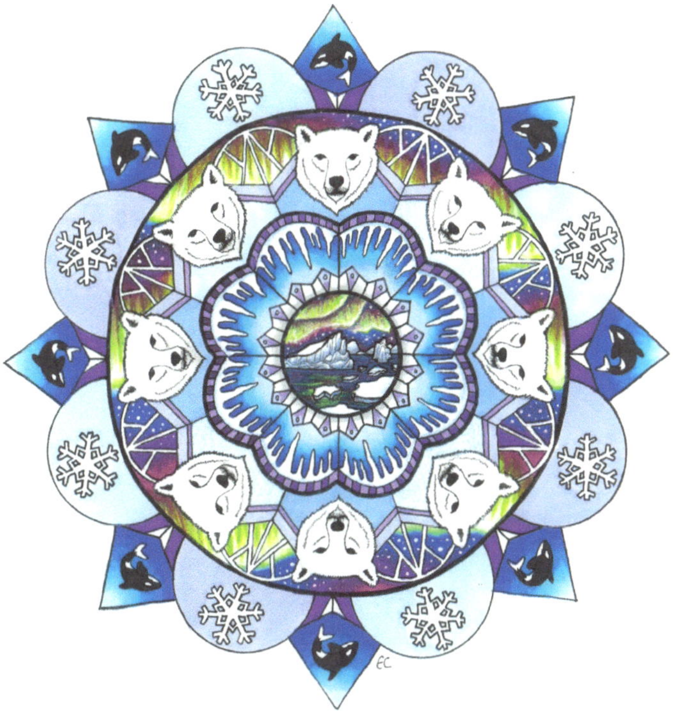

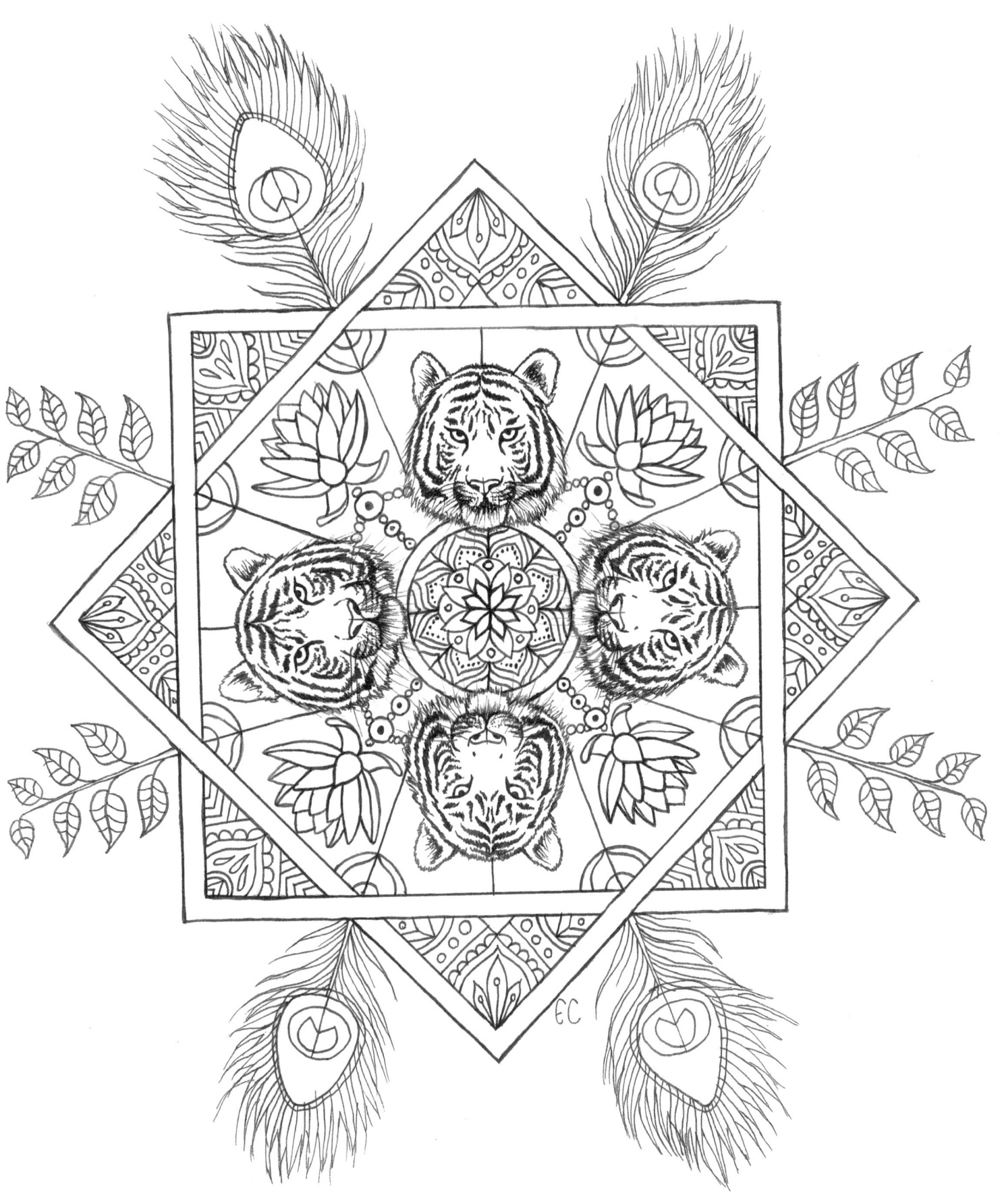

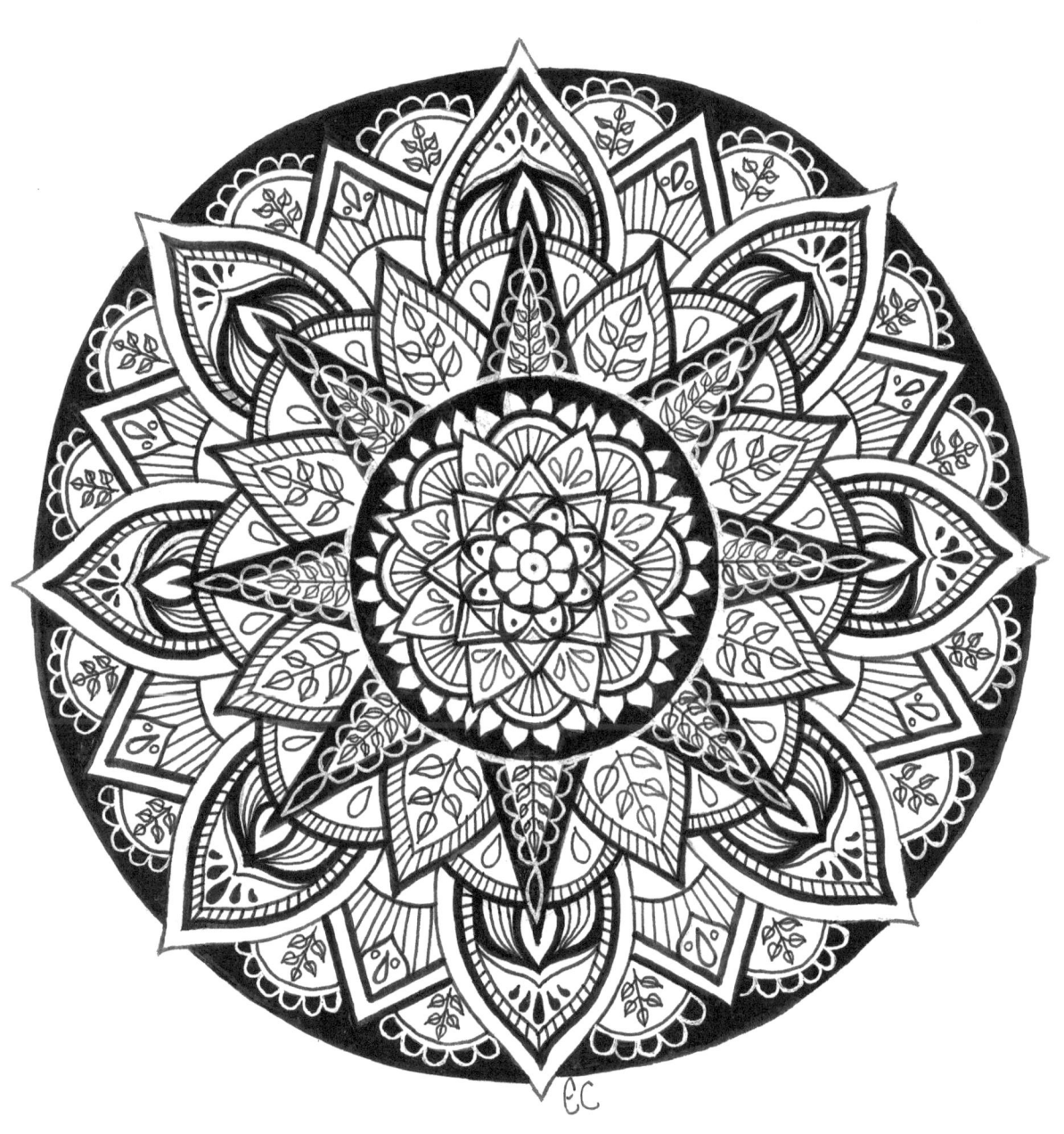

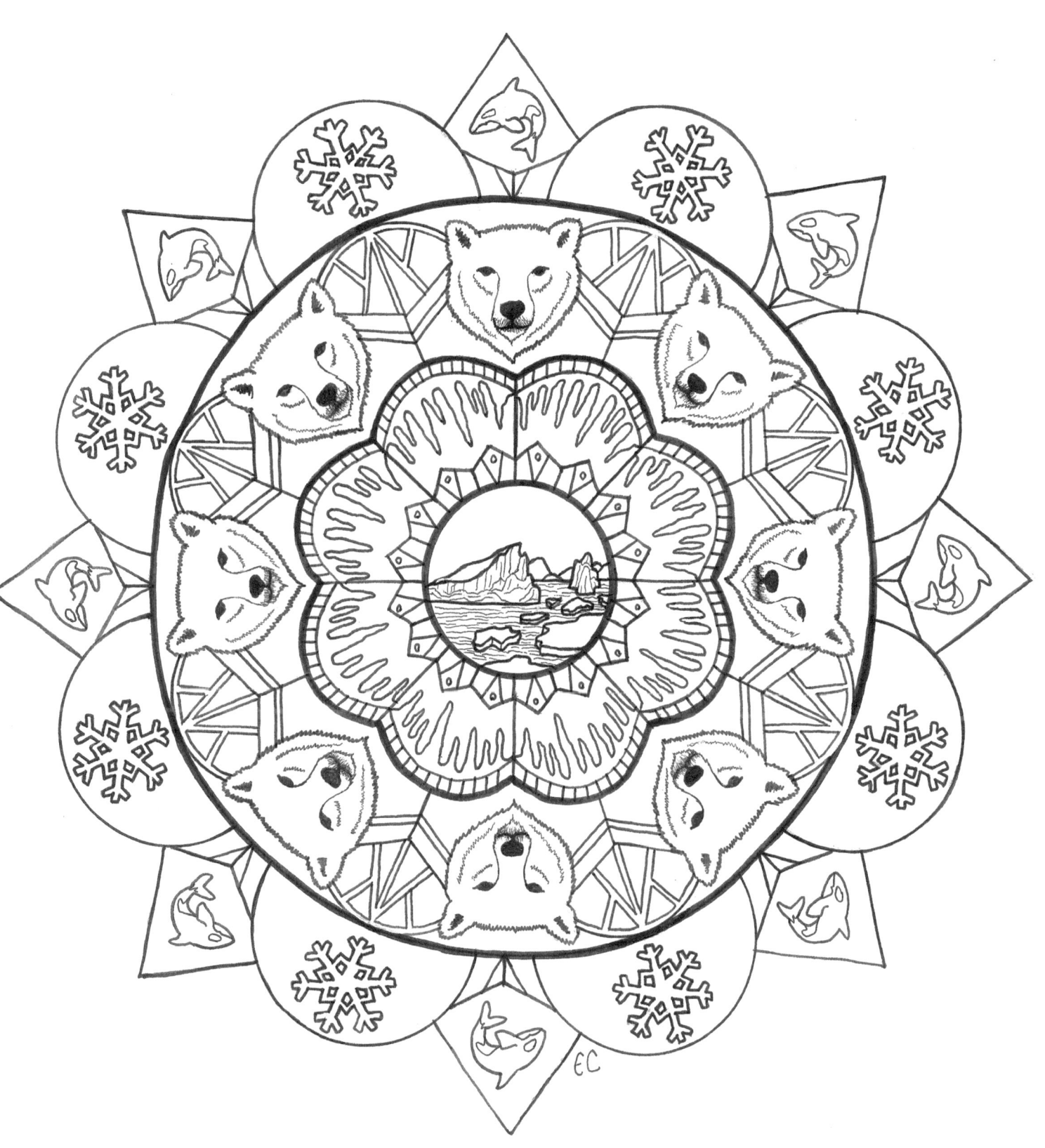

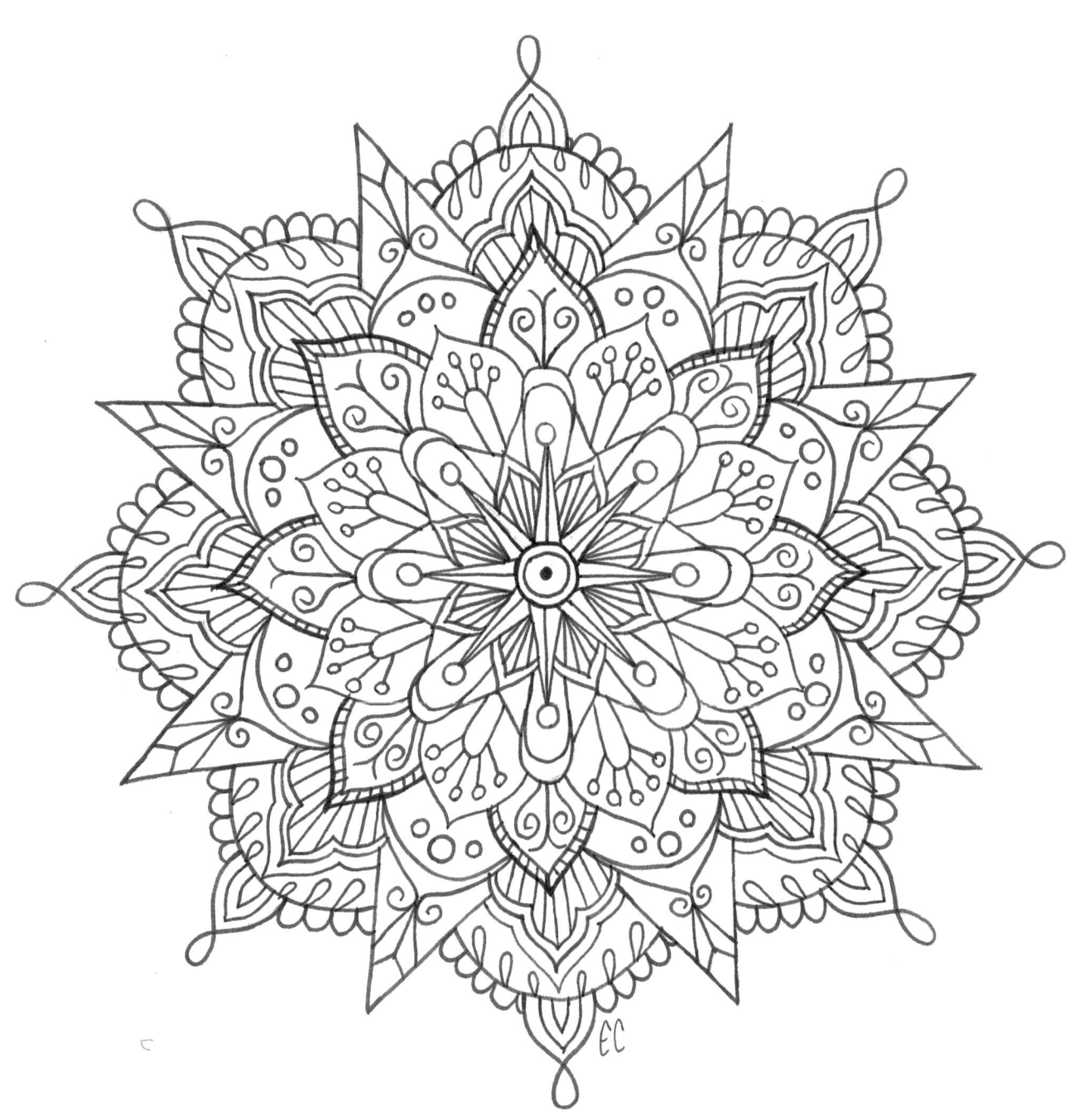

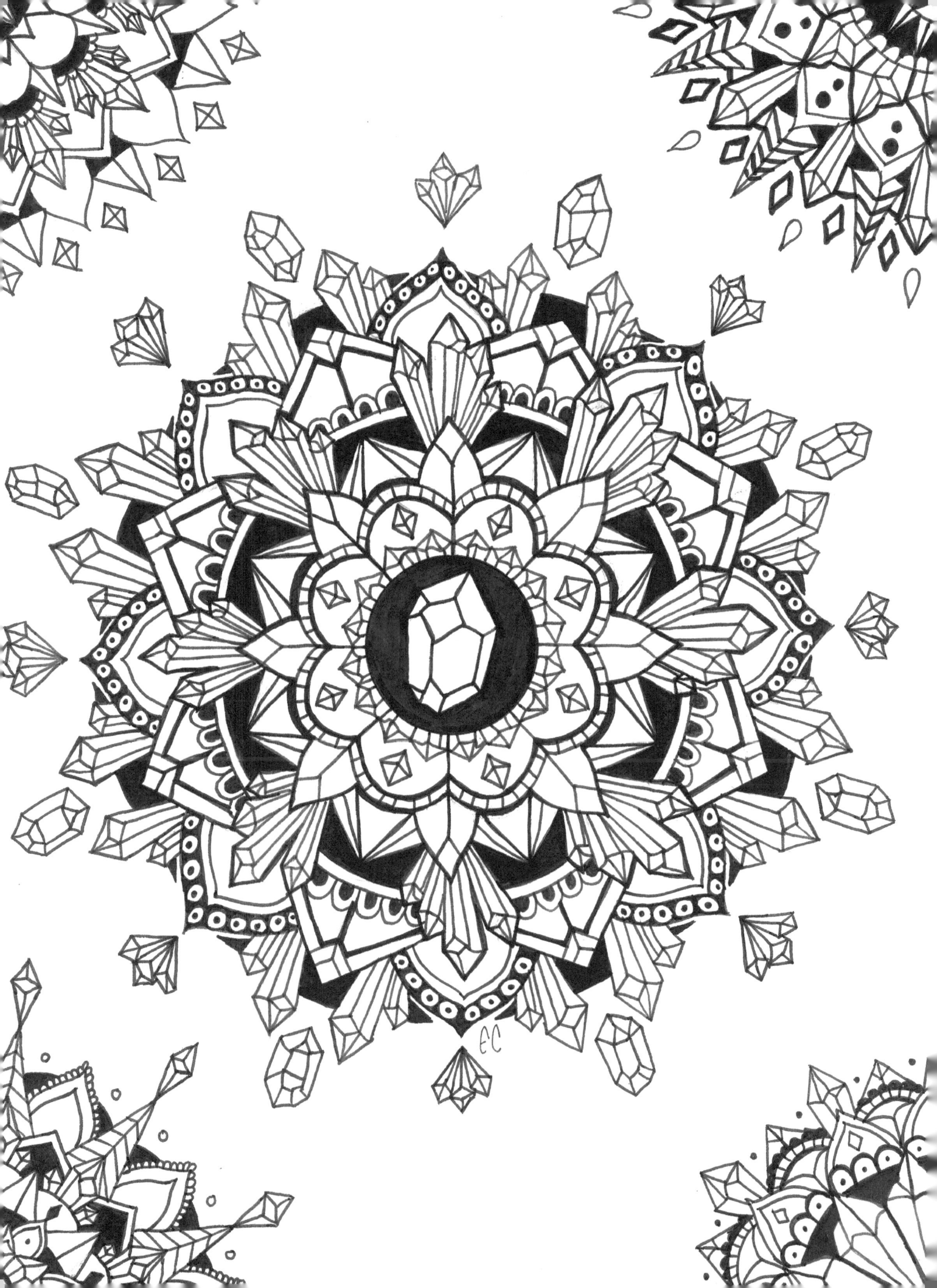

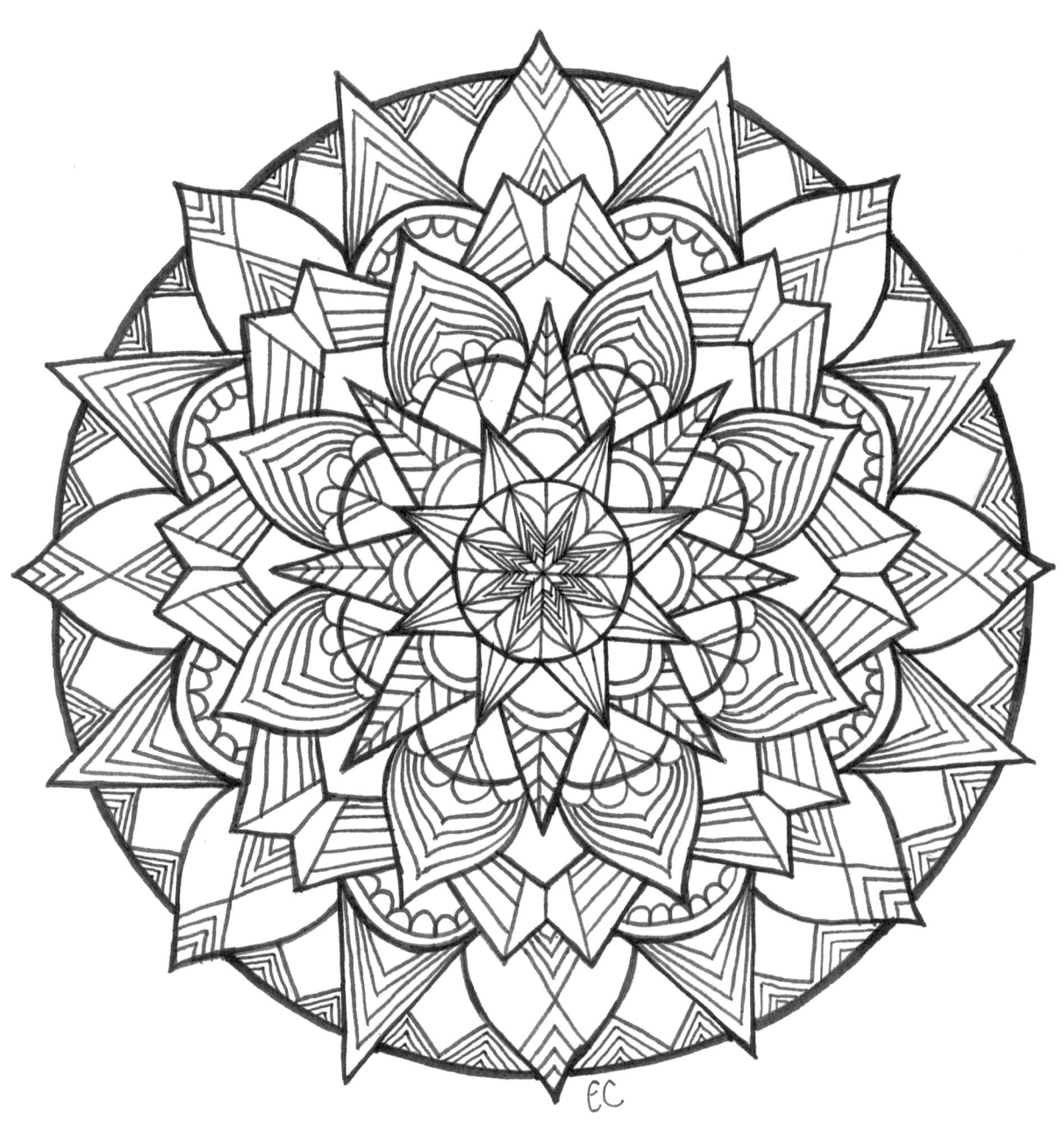

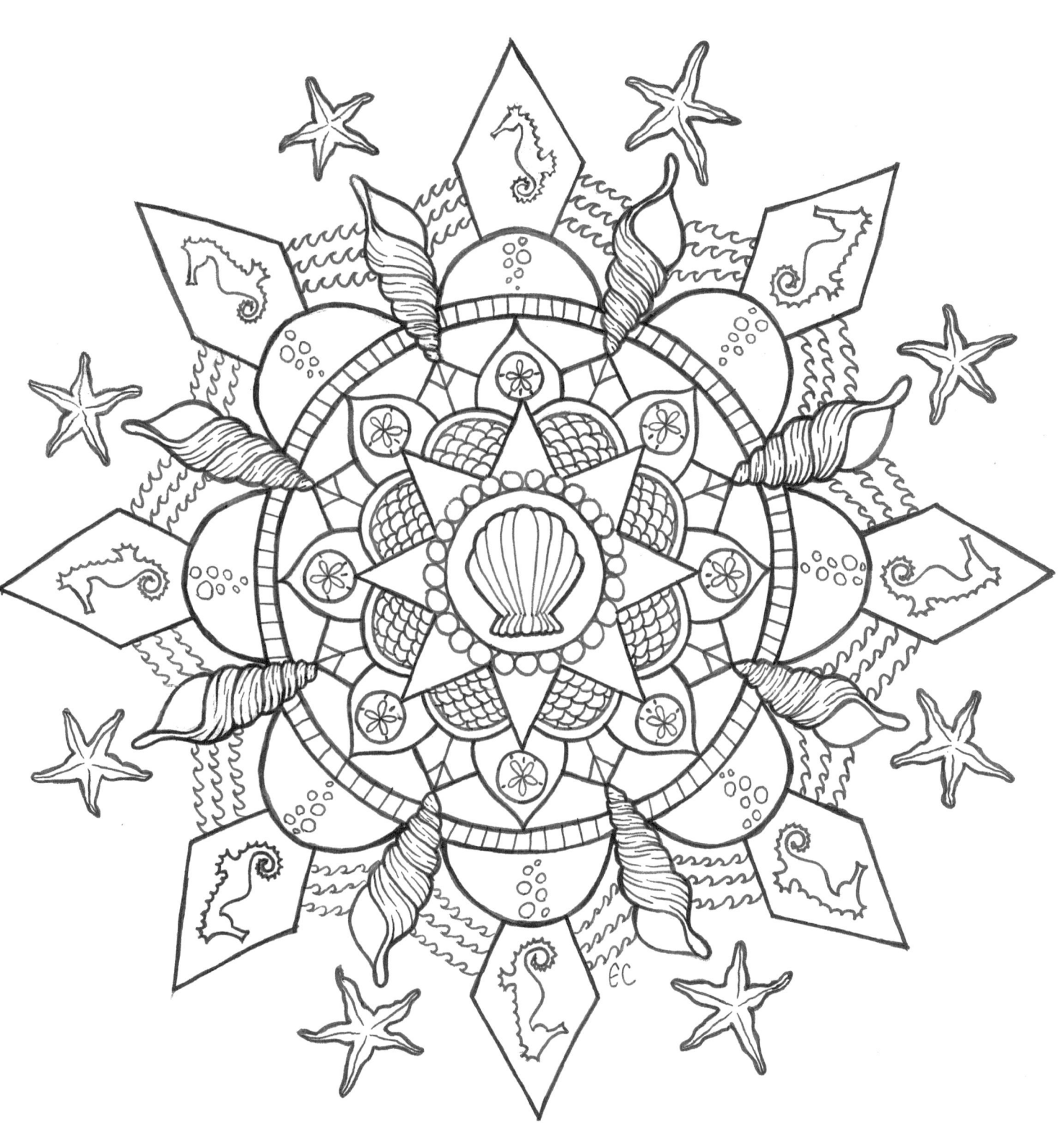

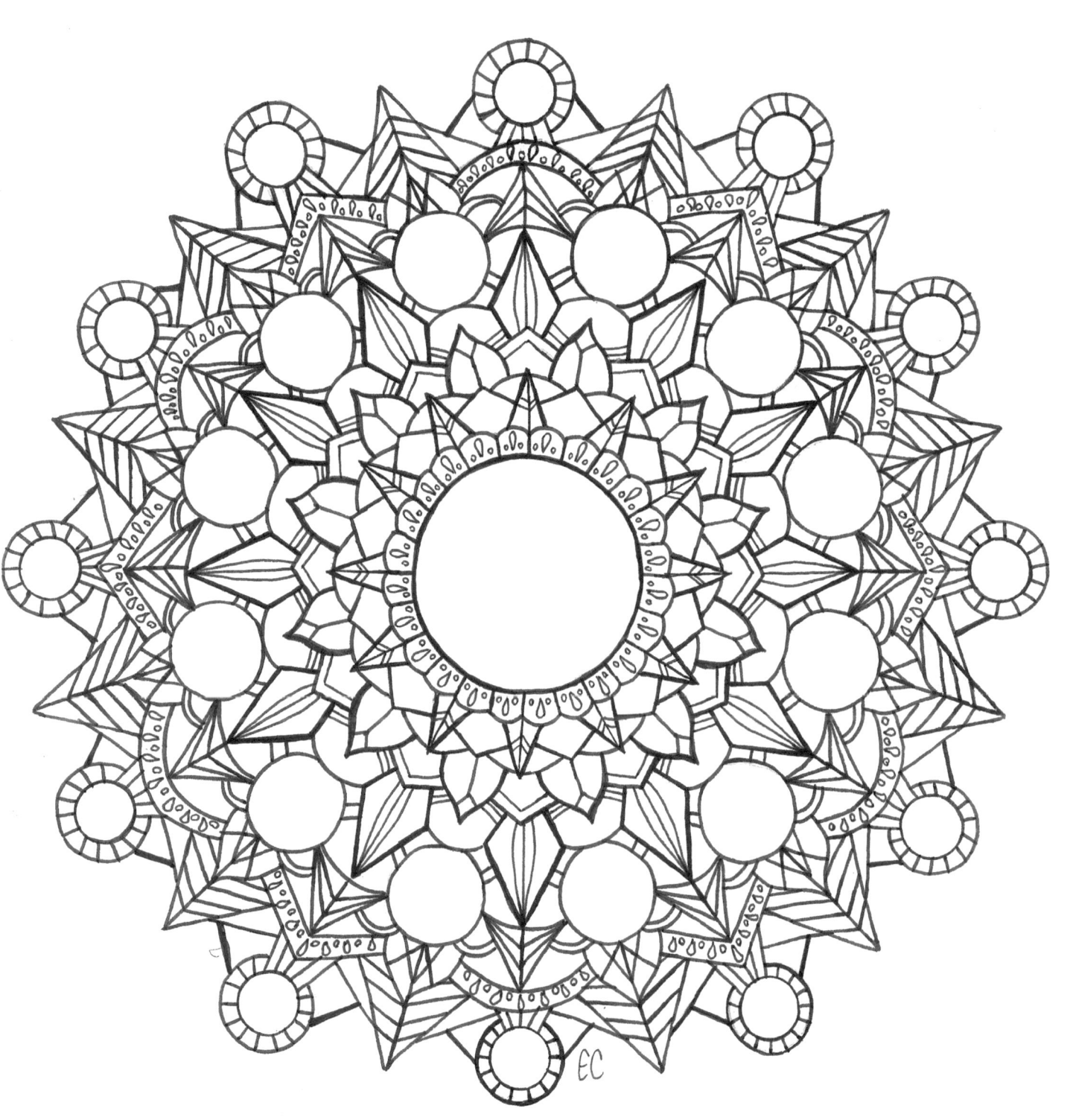

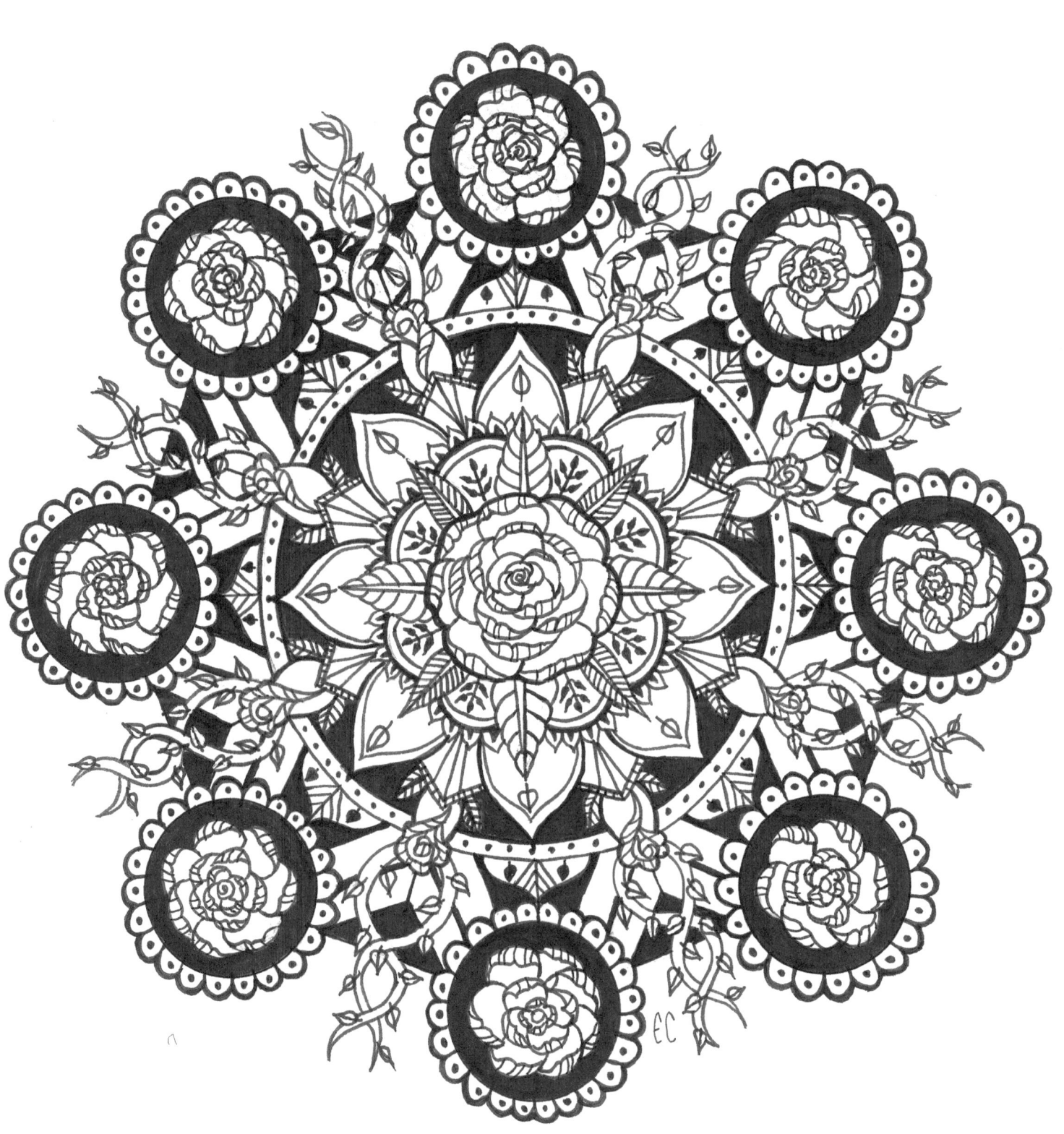

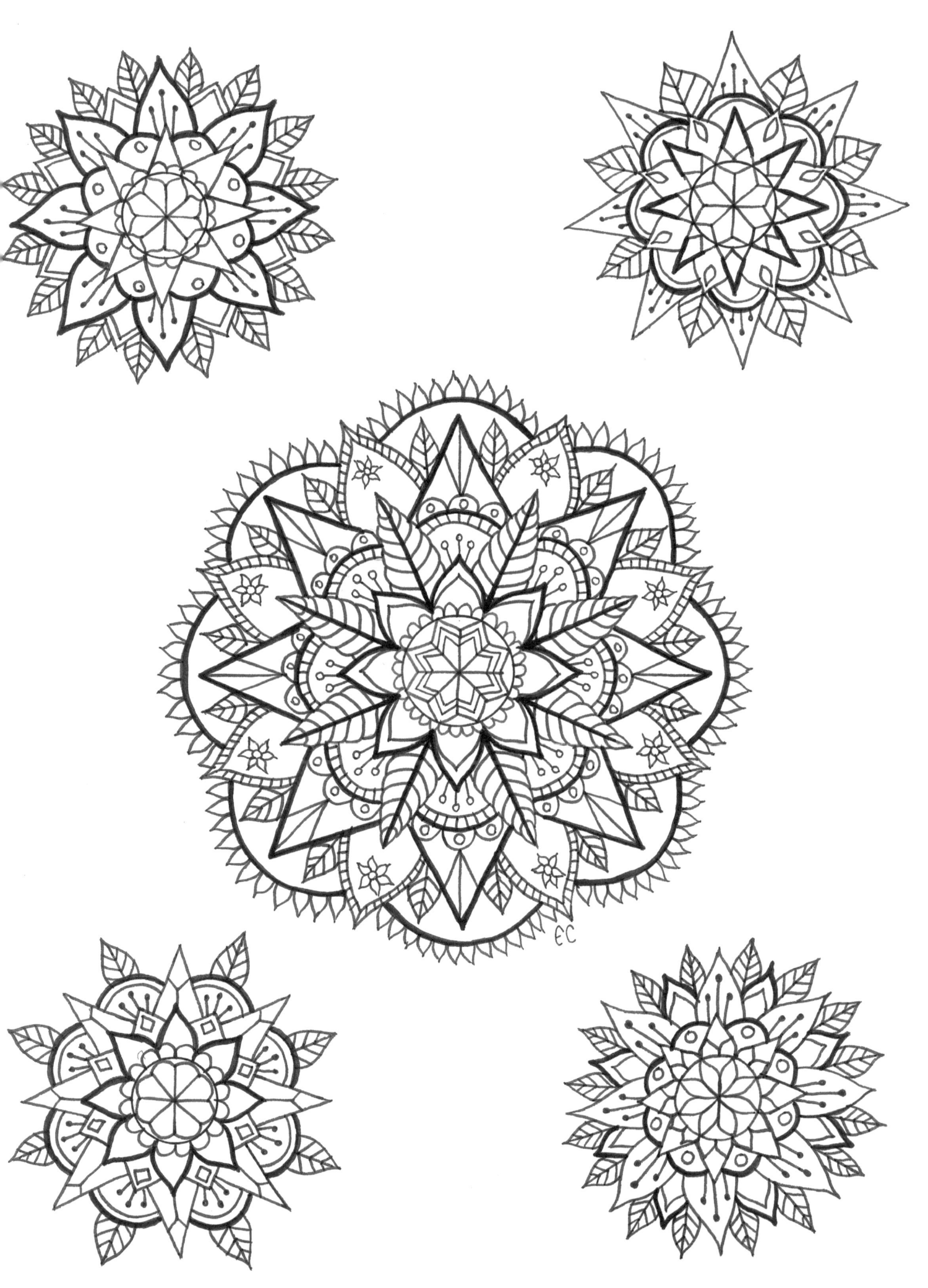

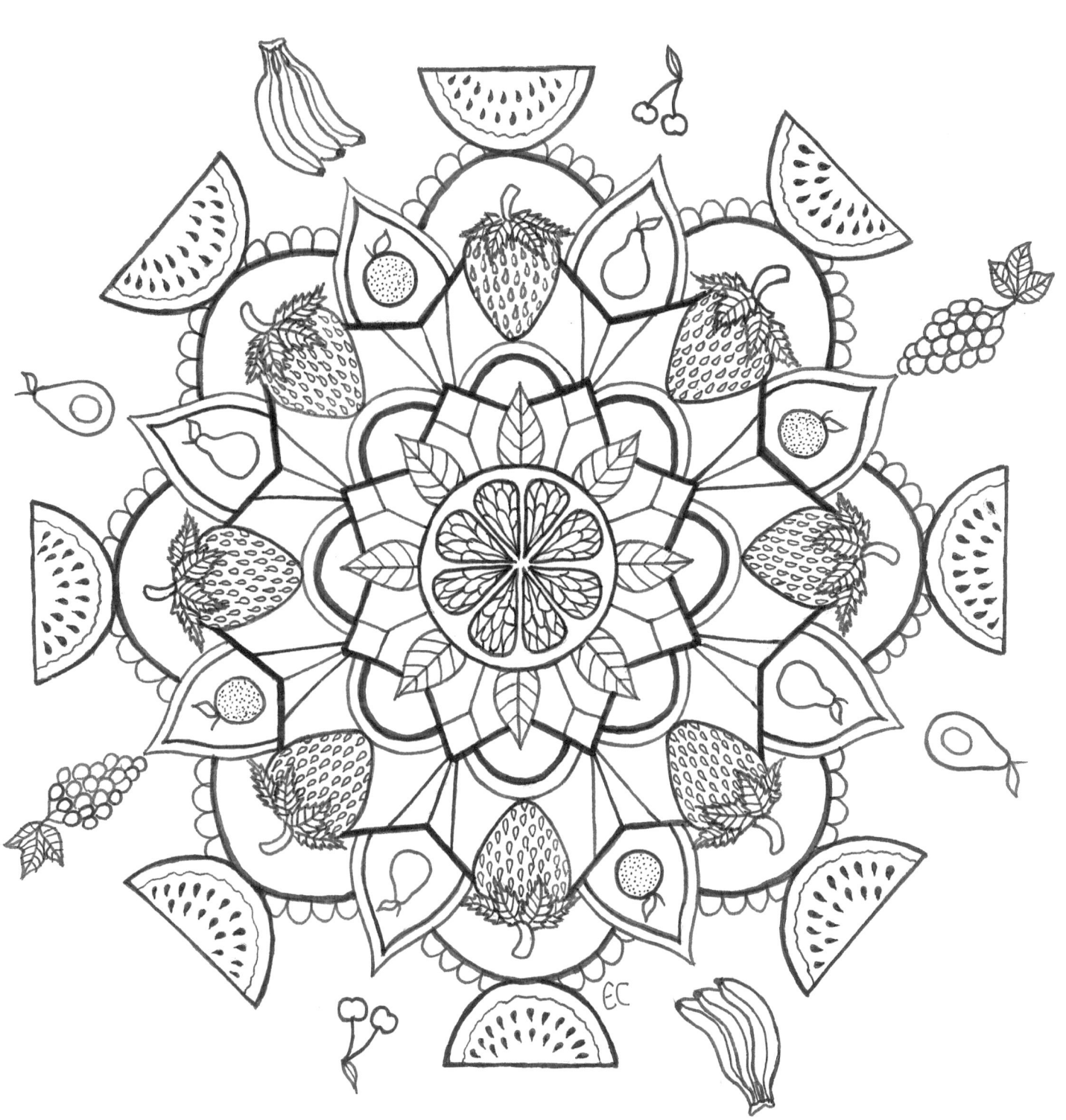

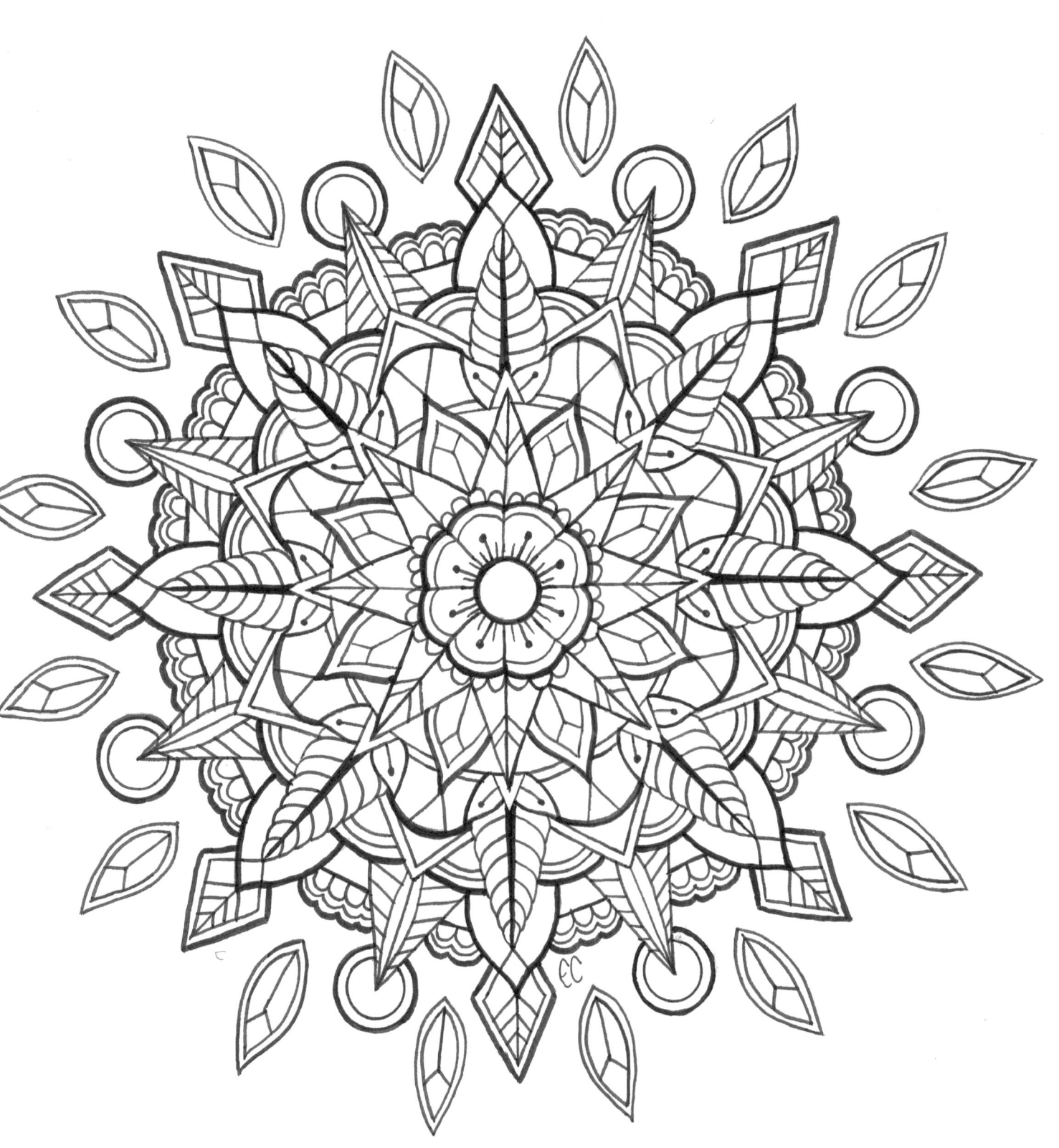

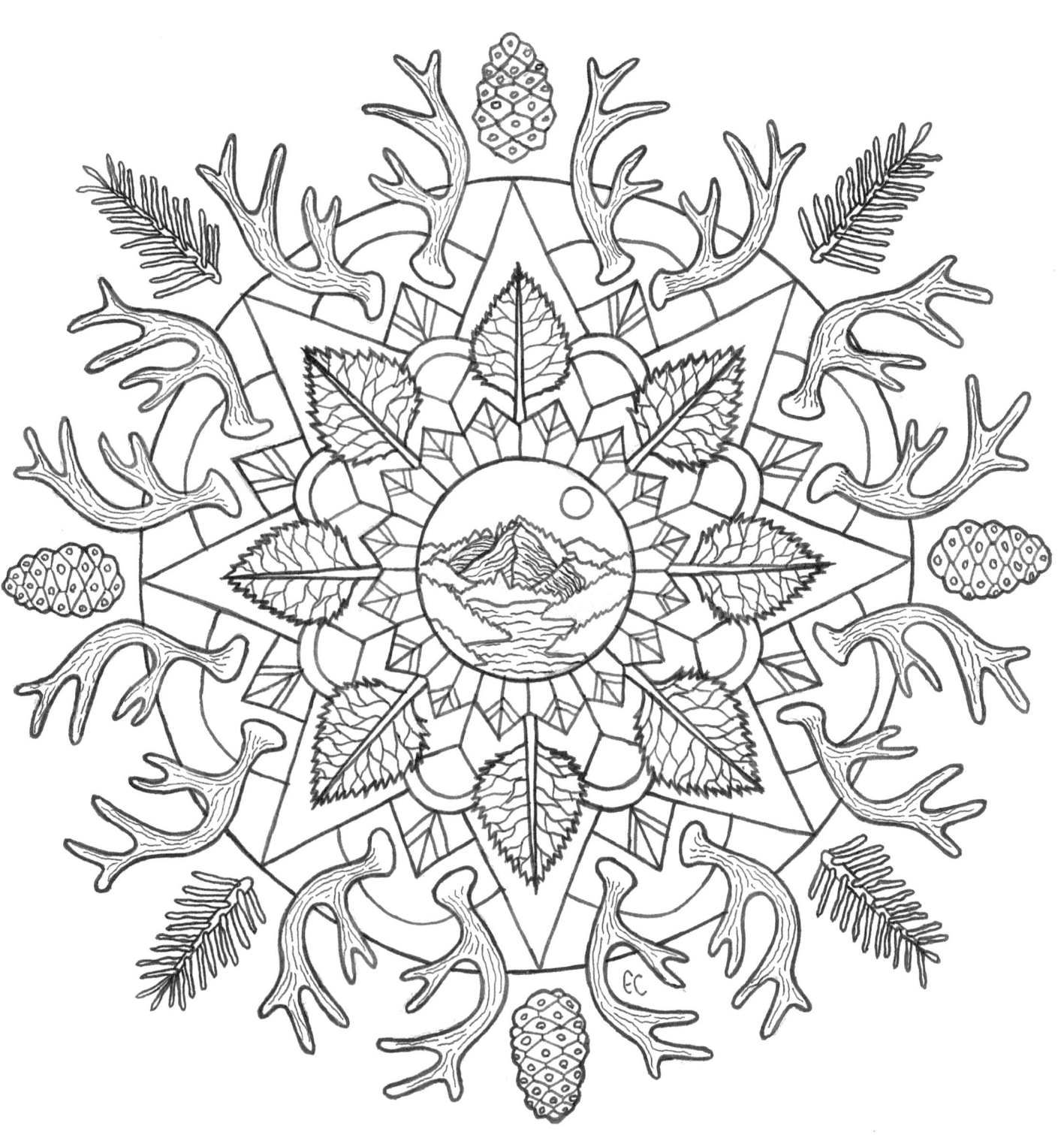

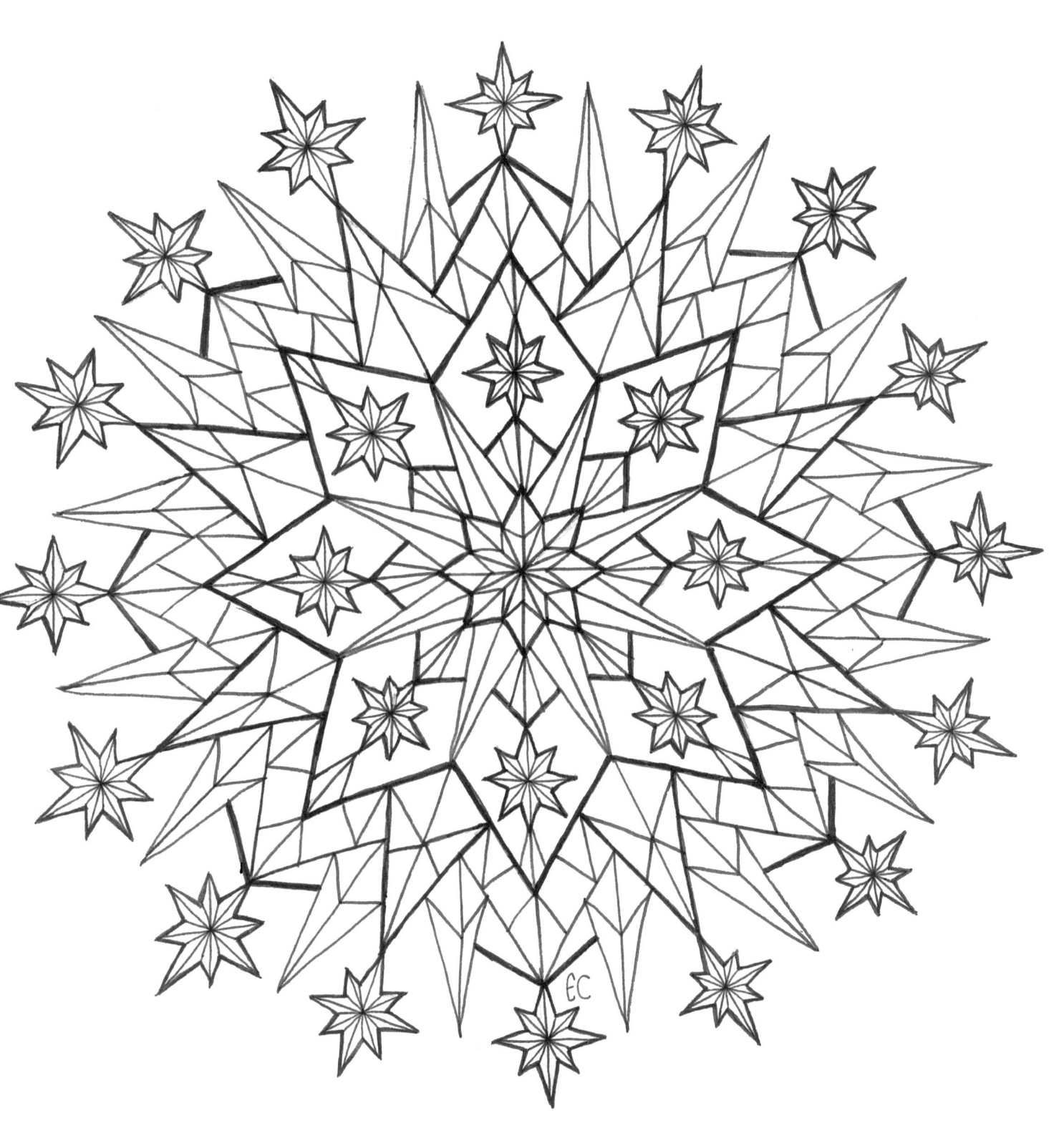

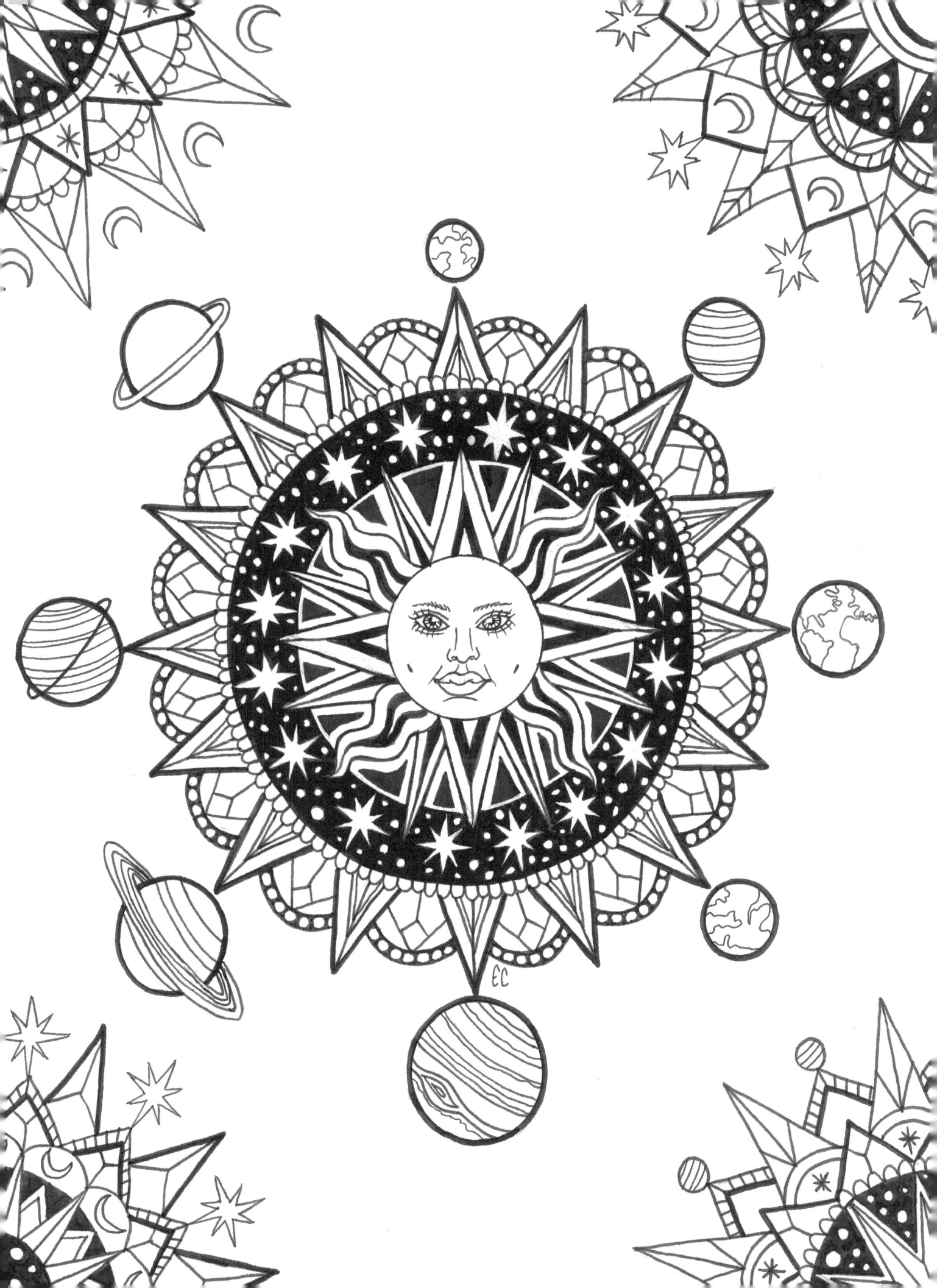

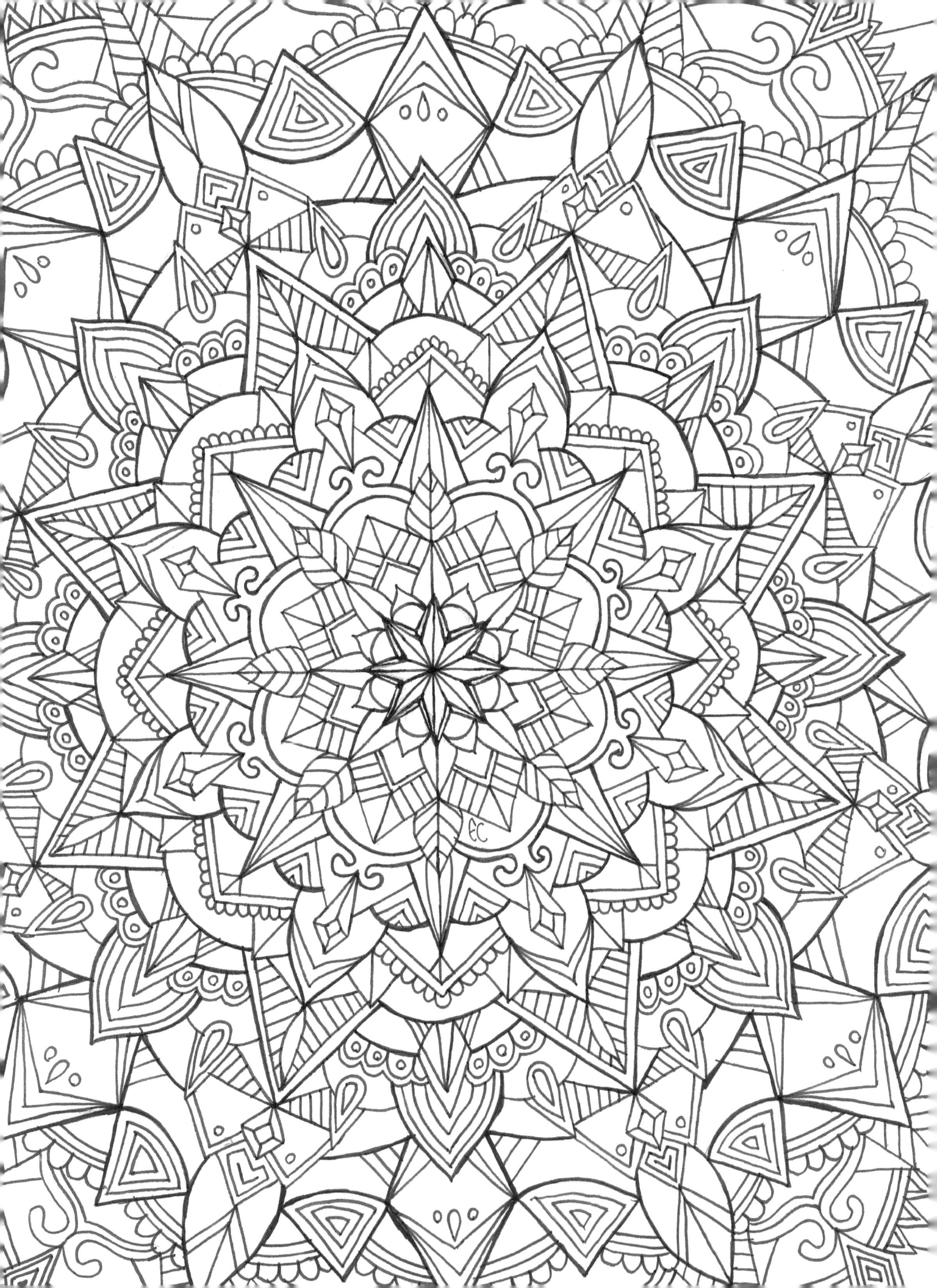

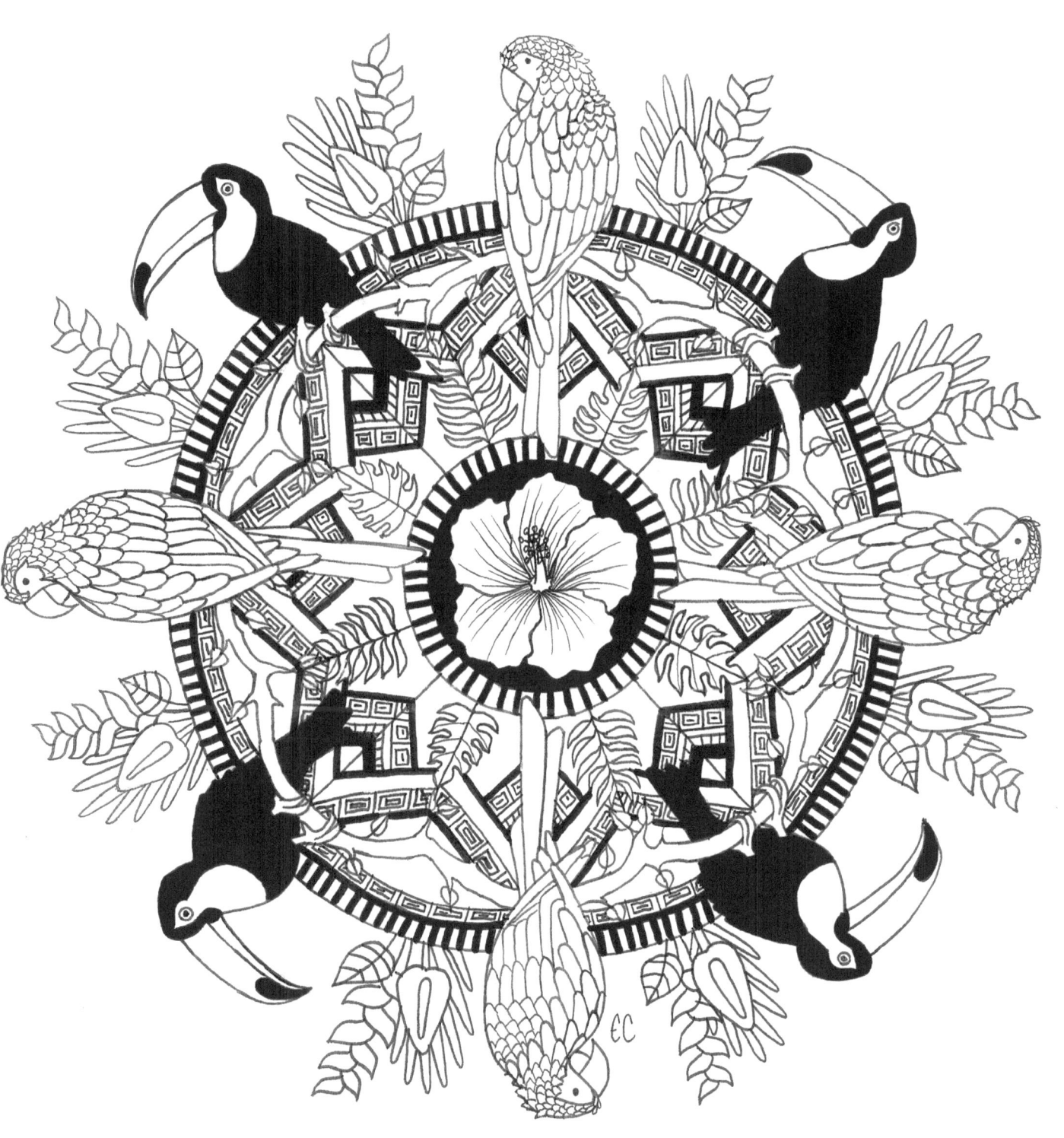

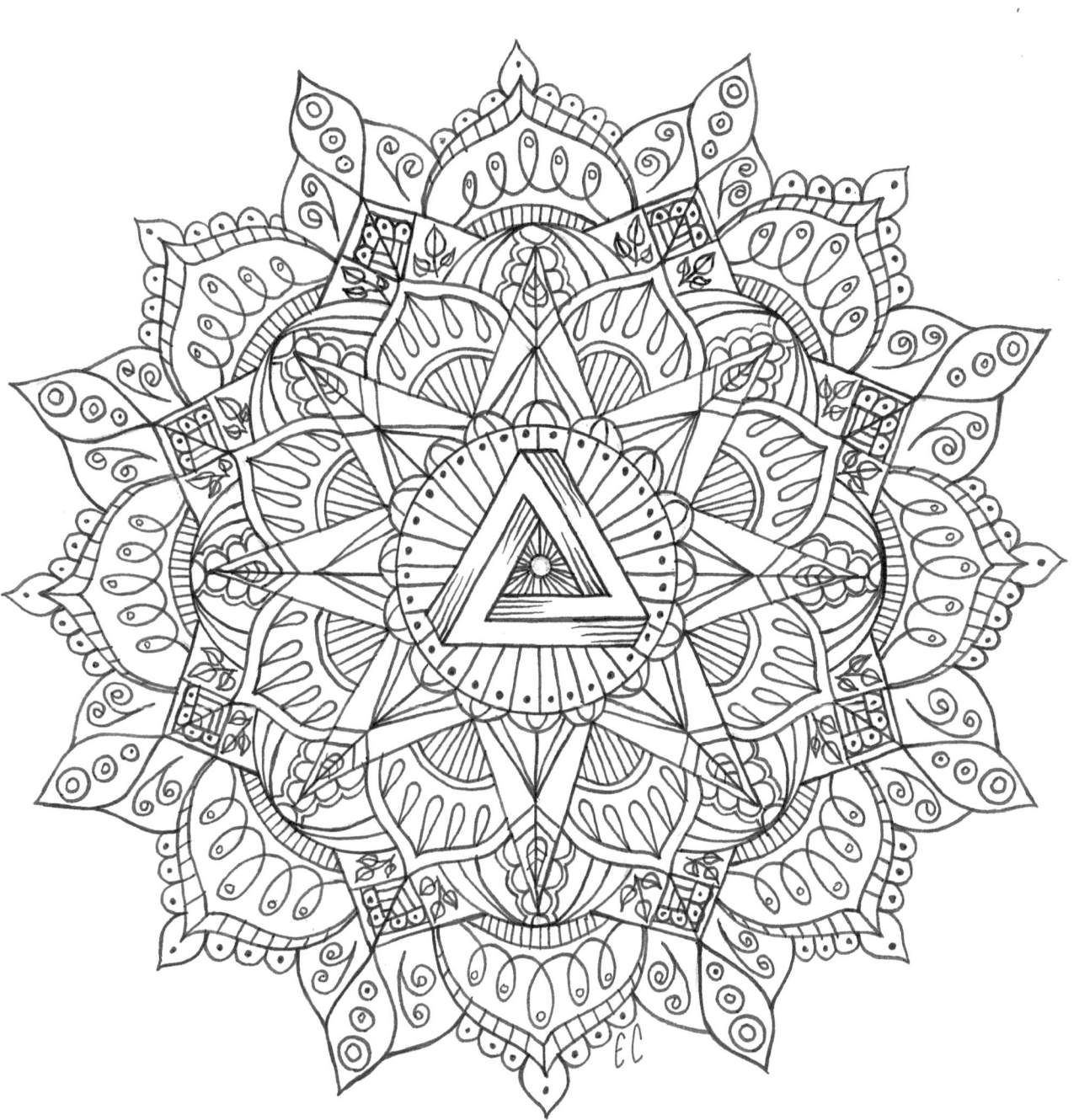

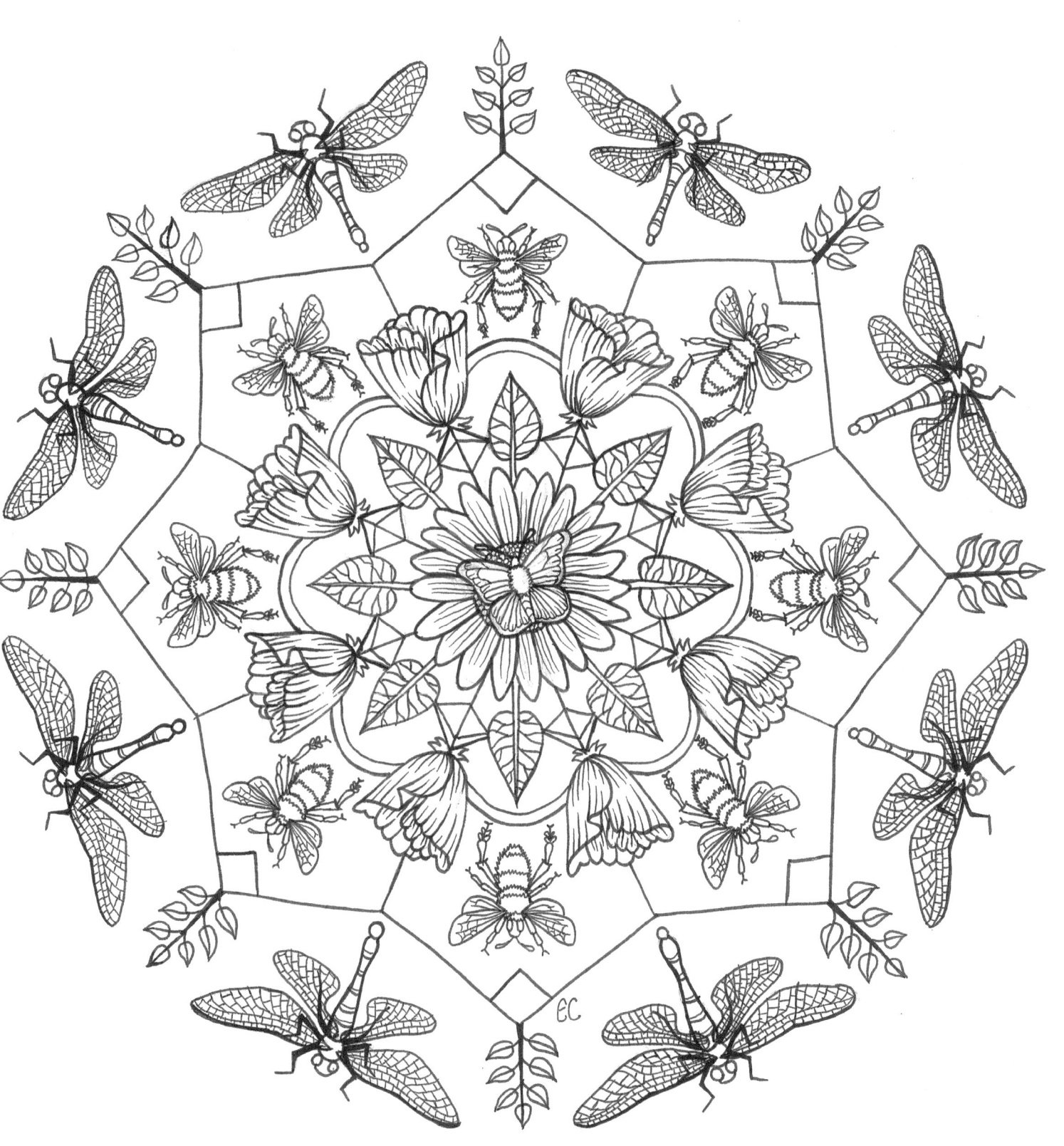

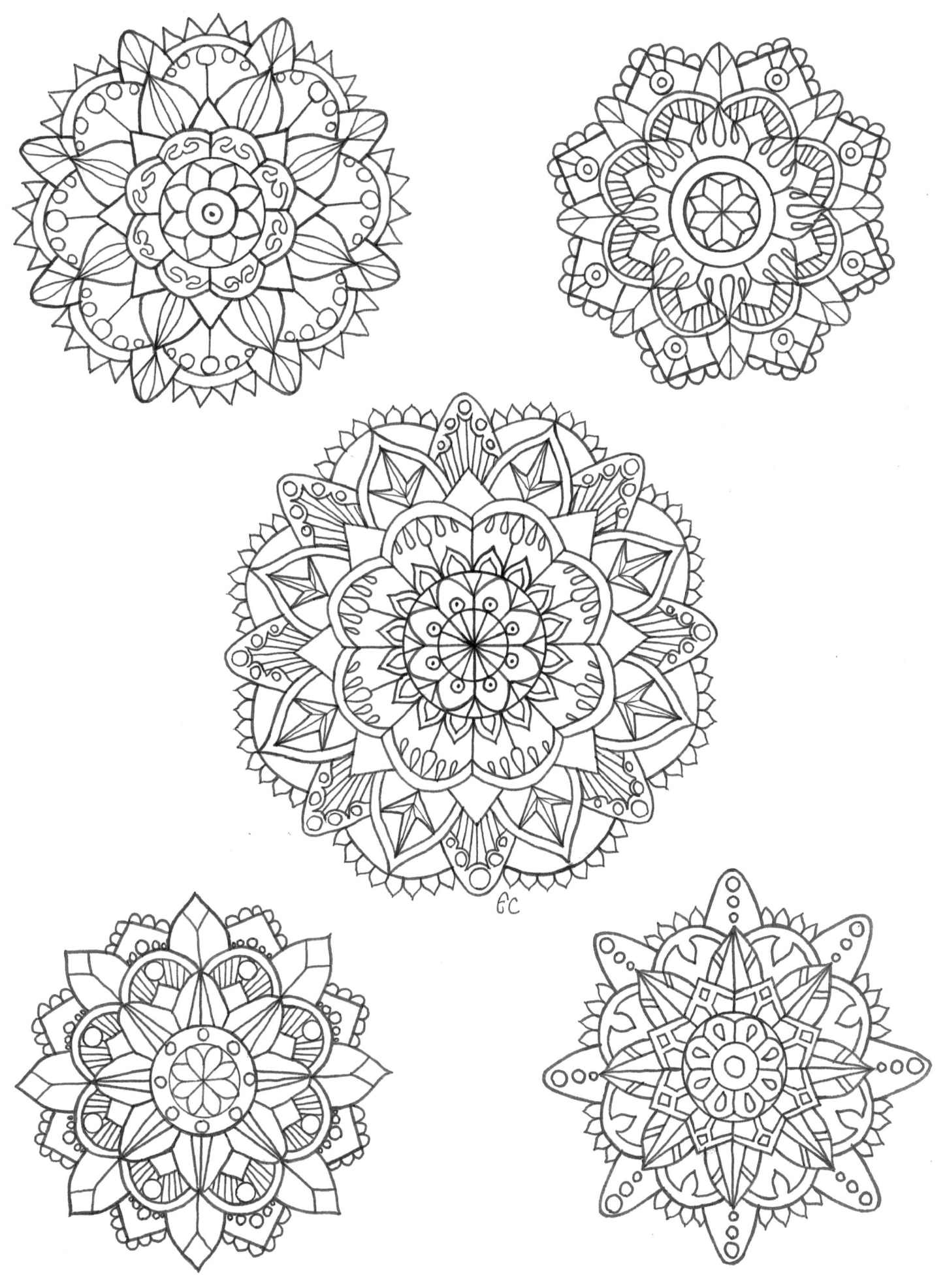

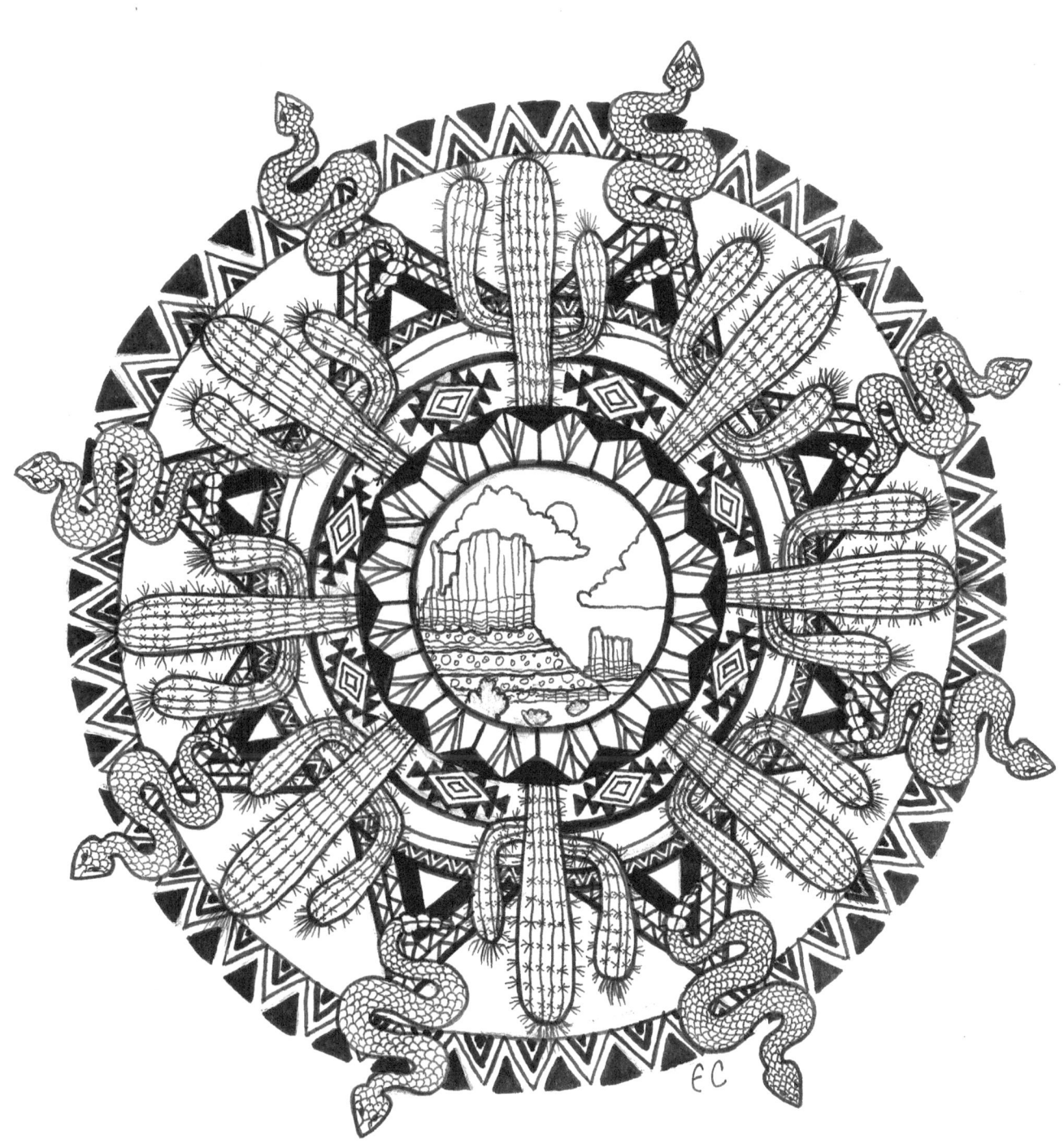

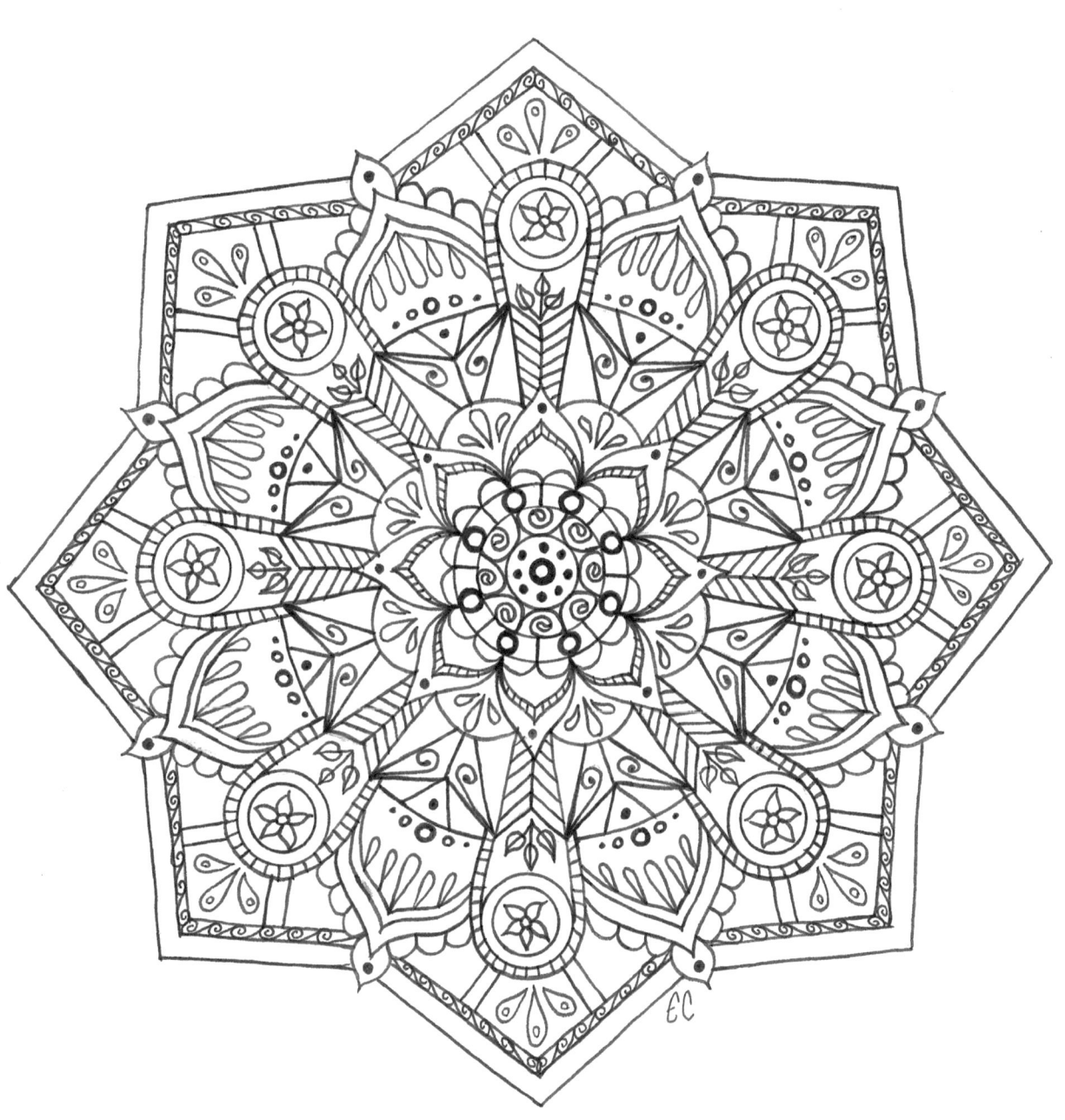

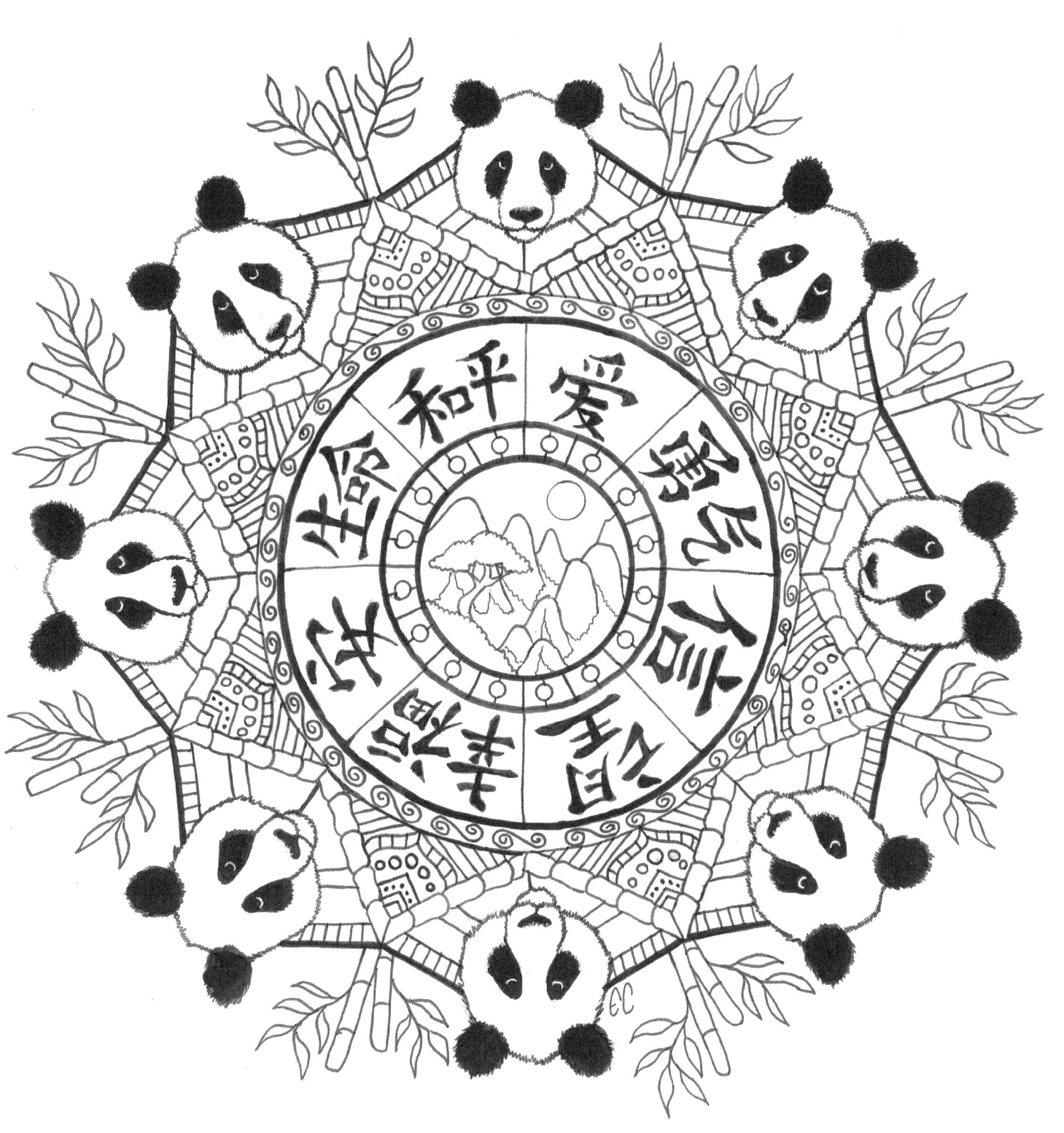

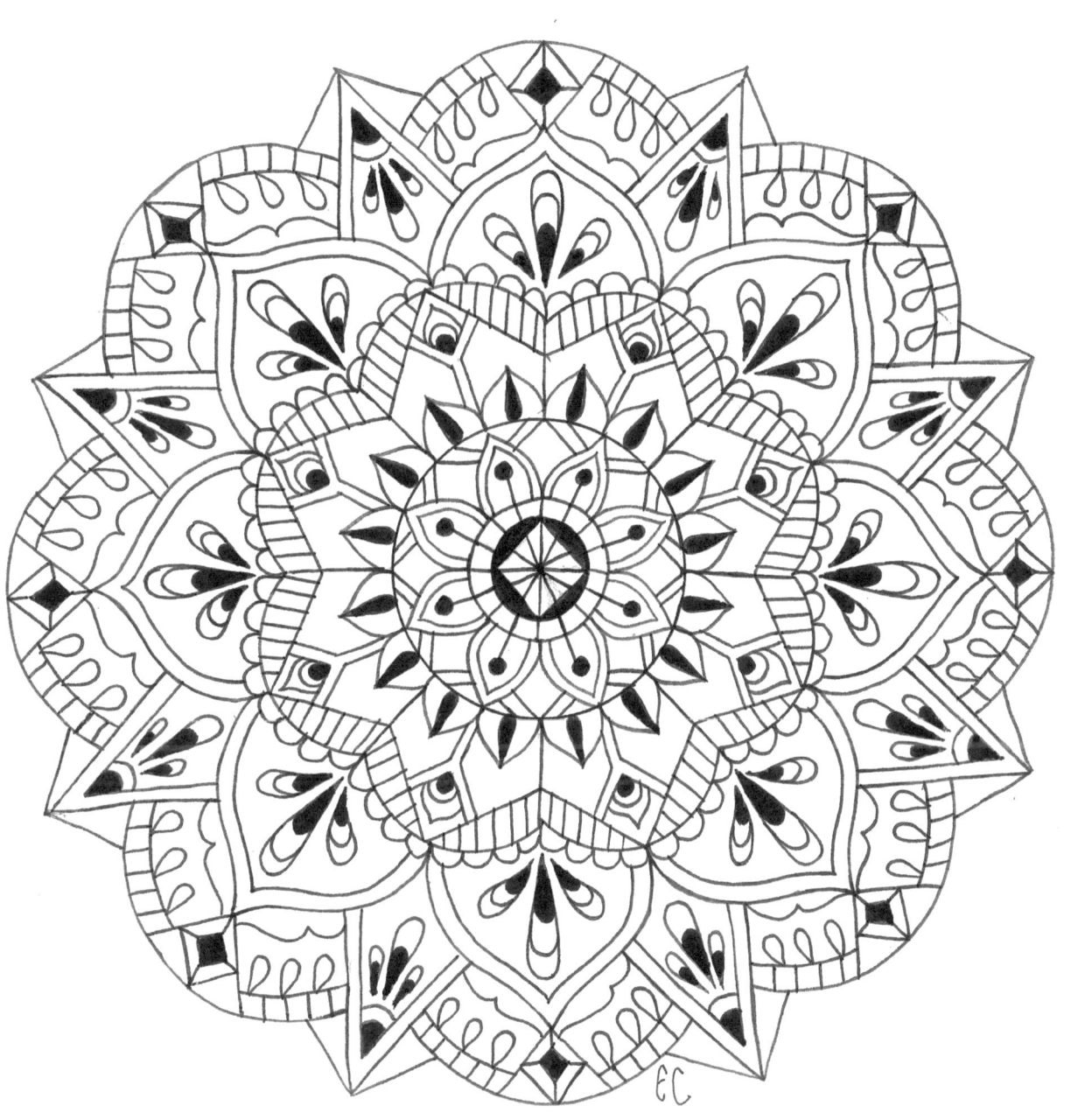

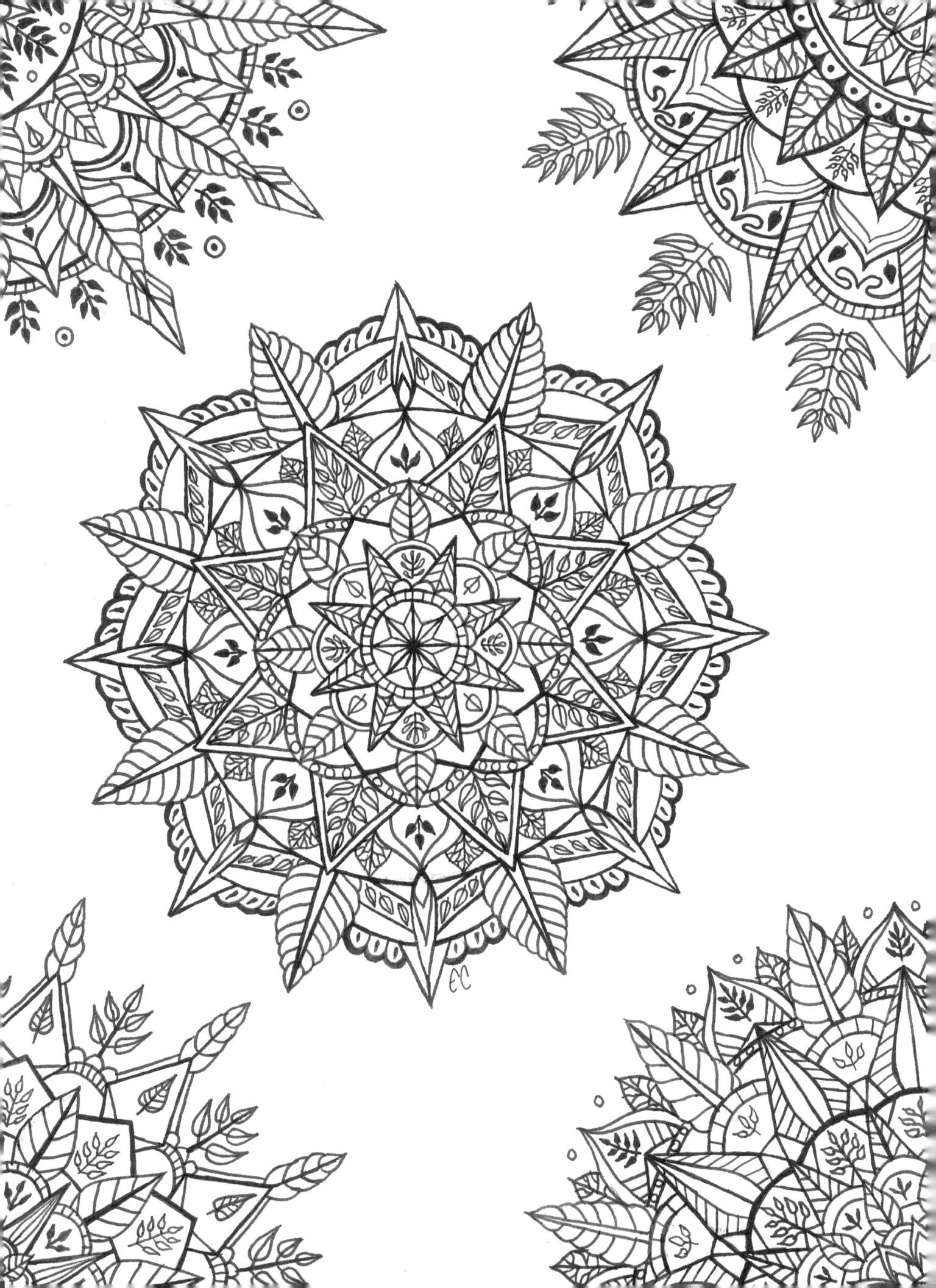

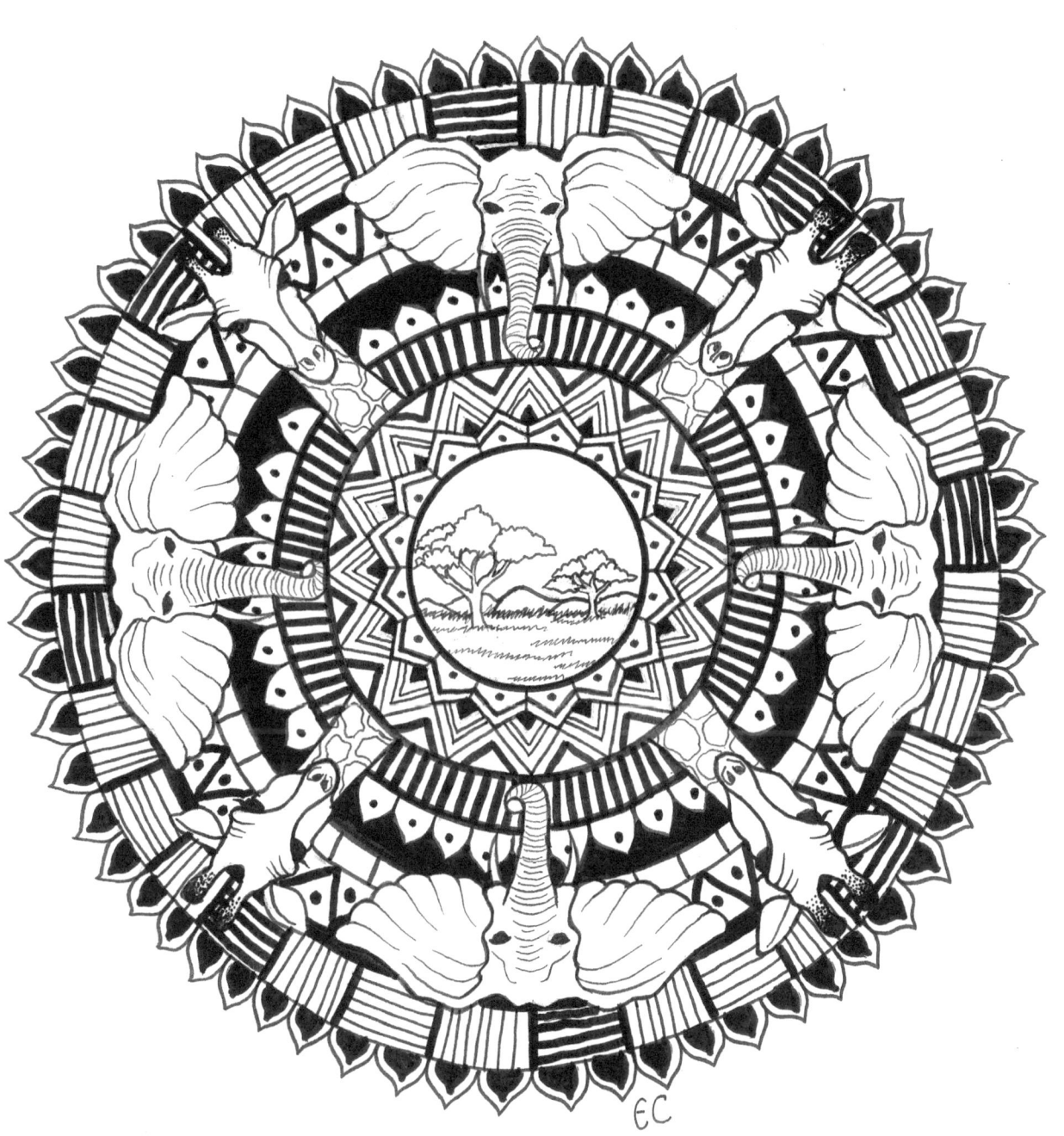

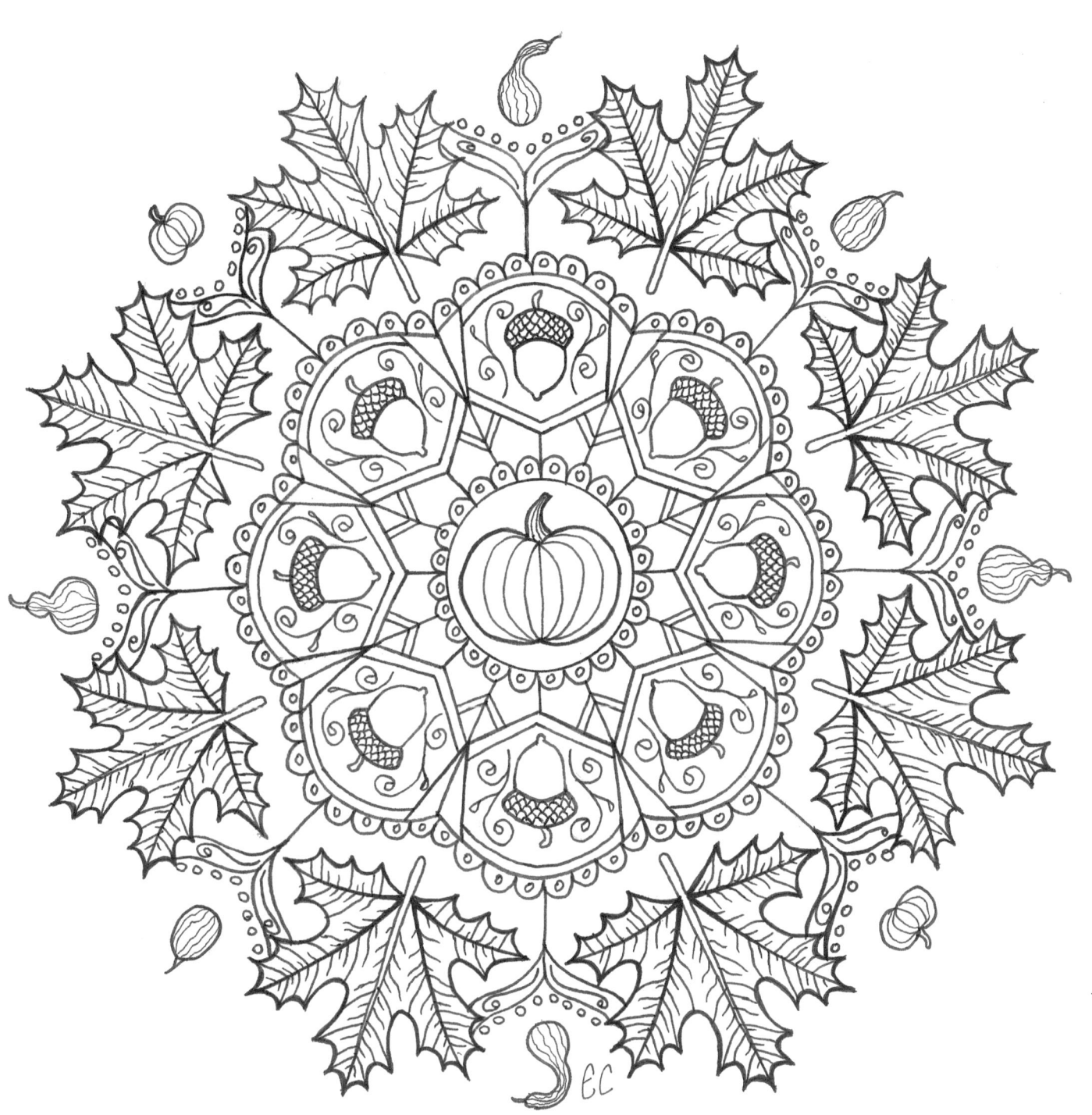

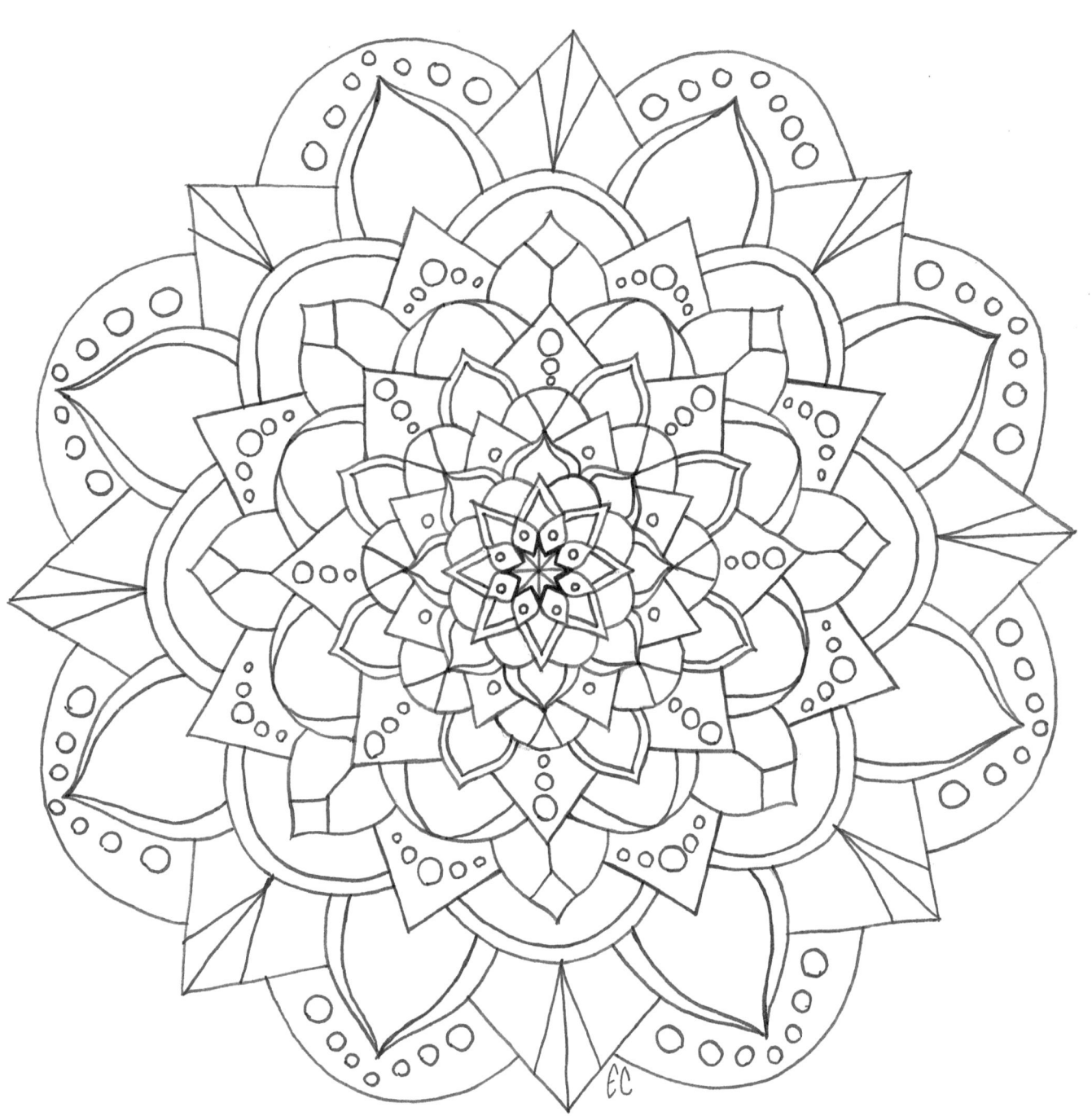

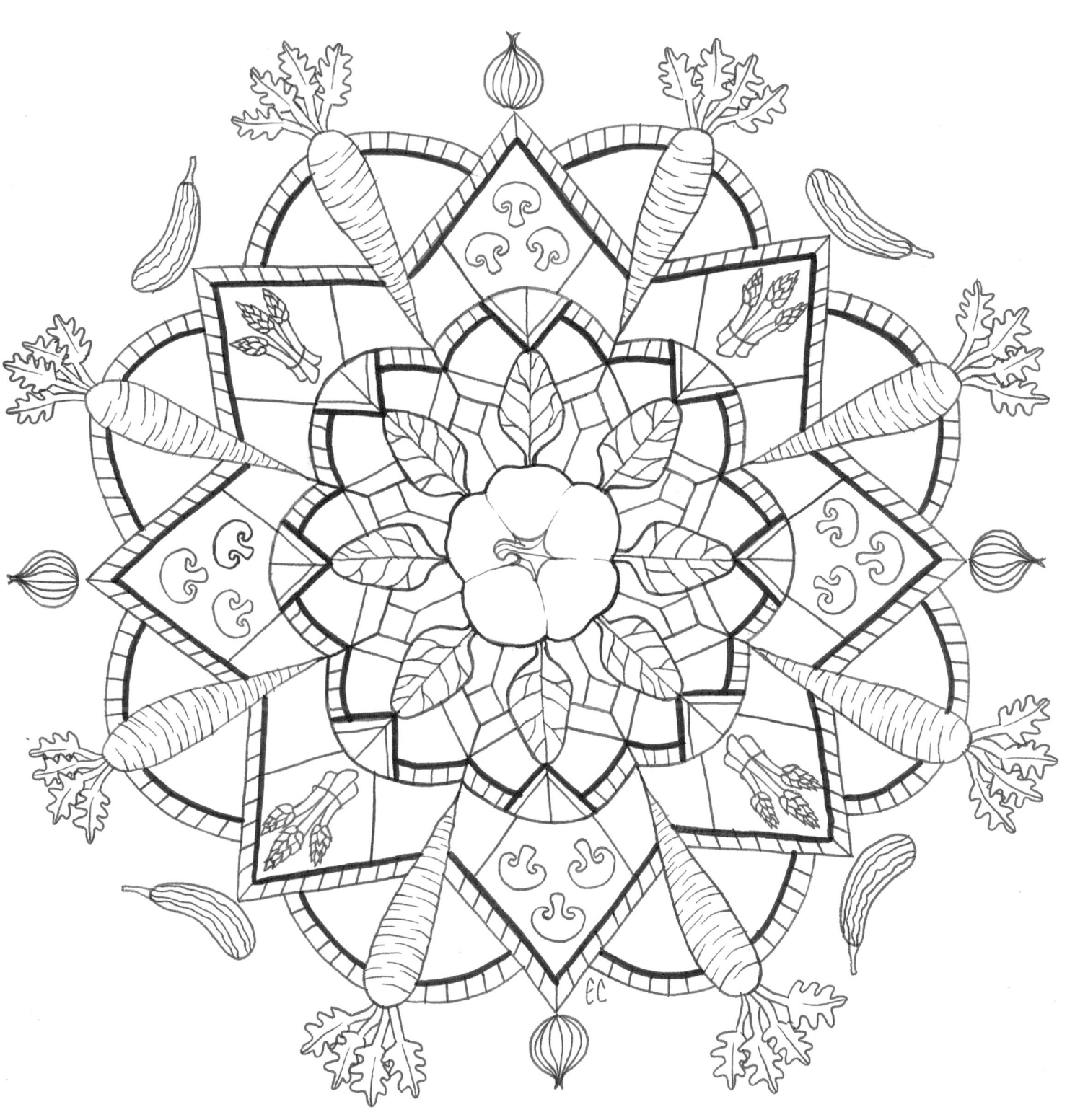

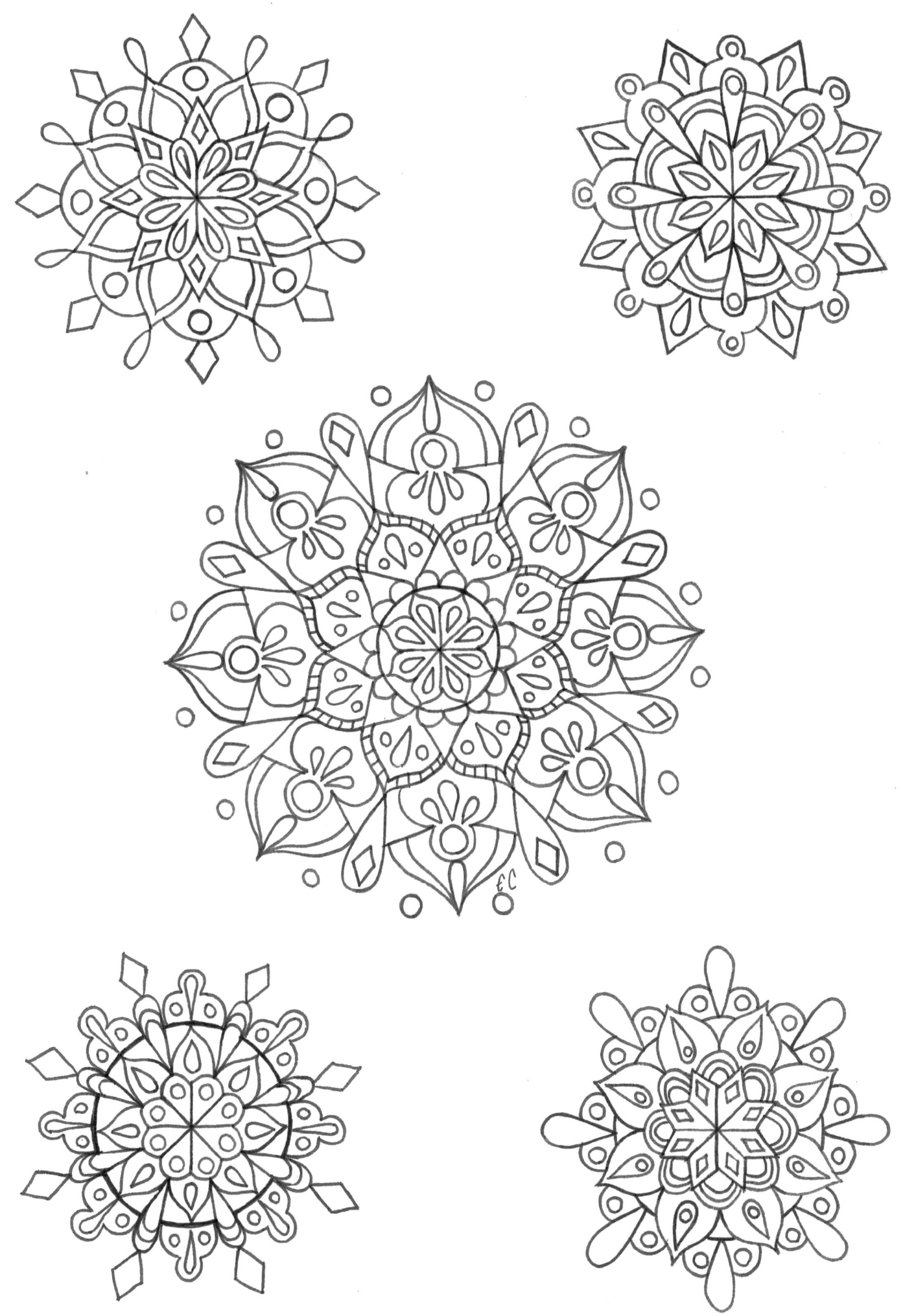

Color Gradient Bars

EXPERIMENT WITH SHADING AND COLOR SCHEMES, AS WELL
AS RELIEVE STRESS WITH THE COLORING BARS BELOW.

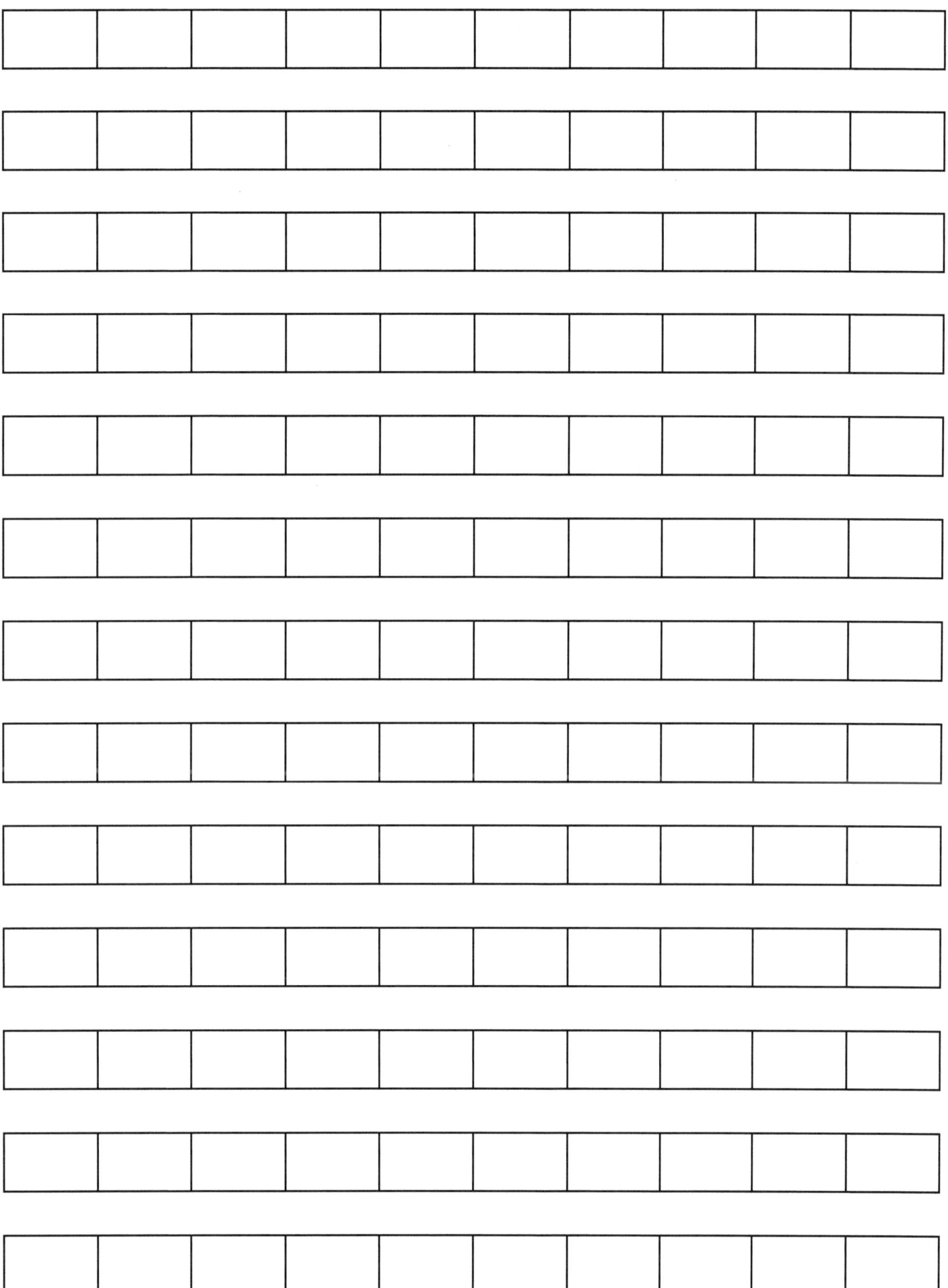

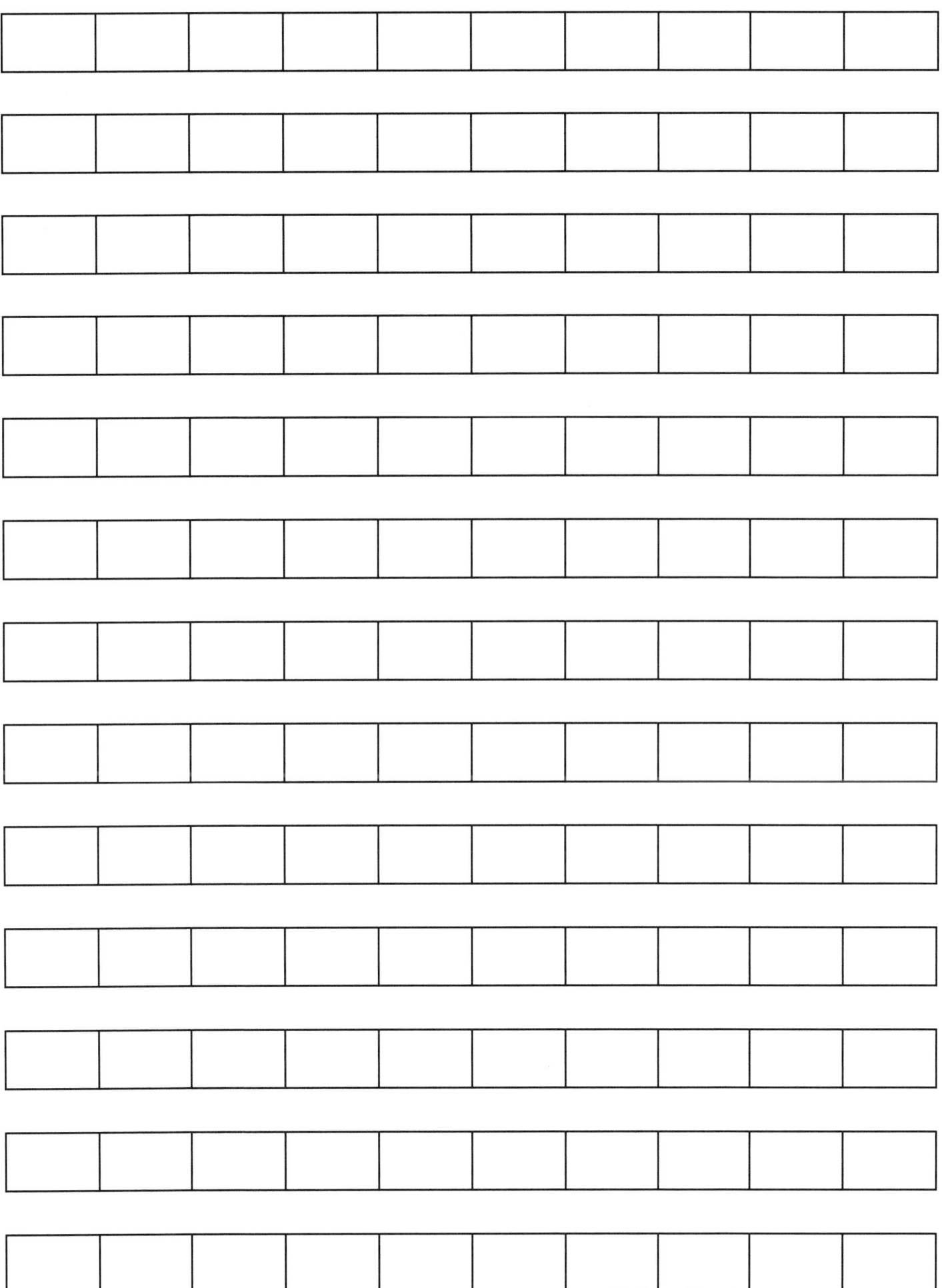